How Do I Live Single Again?

Michelle Bridges Harper

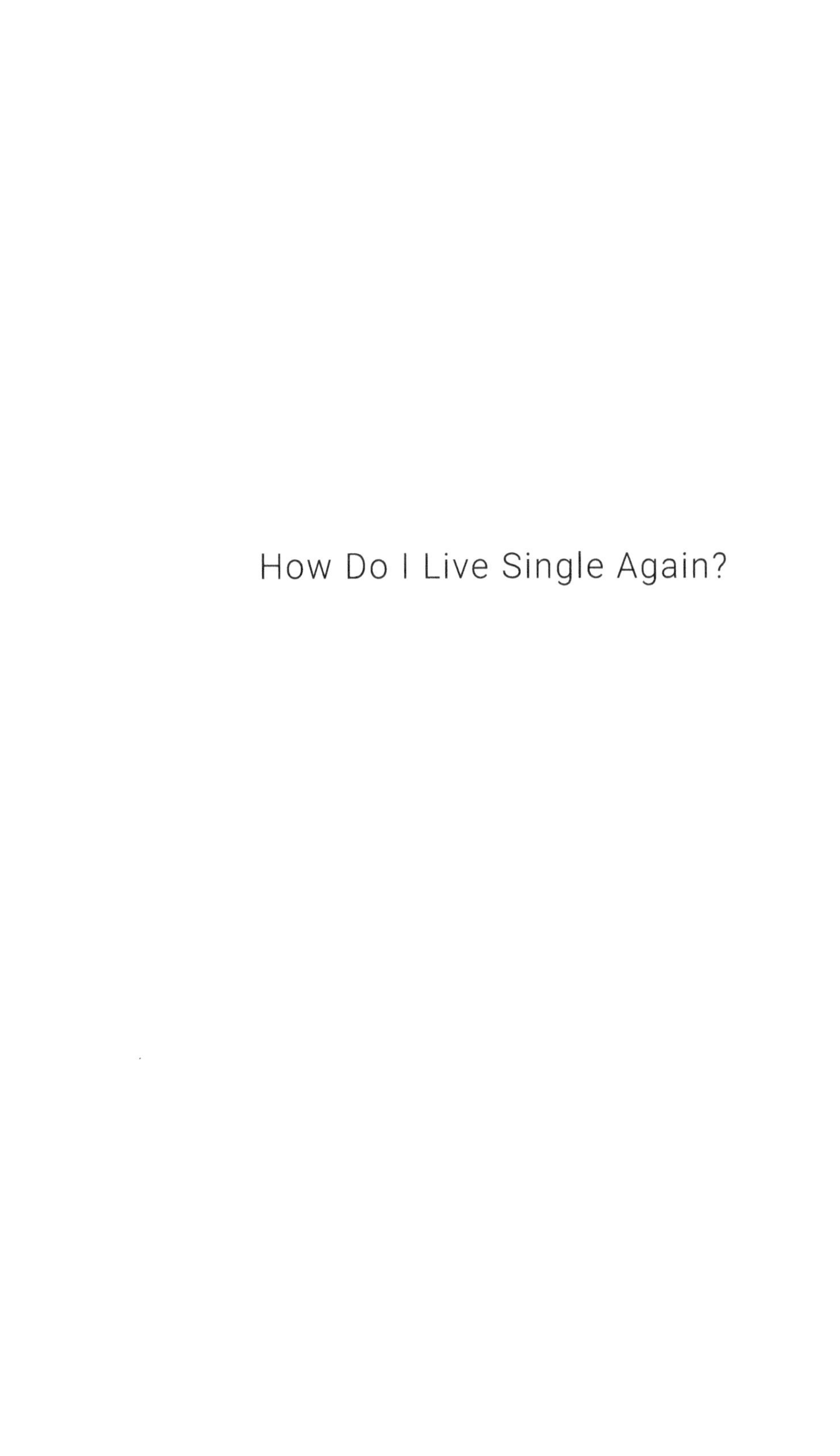

How Do I Live Single Again?

First Printing, 2026.

A special dedication to my friend, Jean, who gave my very first vote of confidence decades ago when this idea emerged from our conversation. You were the one who let me know, I was *not alone!*

To my incredible single friends who have inspired, encouraged, and given me ammo through way too many years of our single lives together. I could not have done this without your support *and stories!*

A special shout-out to my cousin, Linette. My forever catalyst. I will be always grateful for your text that Super Bowl night. Without you, I'm not sure I would have ever been brave enough to push the Go button.

My deepest gratitude is to Chris, the man who rescued me from living life alone. My biggest fan. Thank you for believing in me, pushing me, cooking late night dinners, listening tentatively to chapter after chapter, graciously handling the painful stories... and respecting the *Busy* light. This book quite literally could not have been completed without you. Thank you for making my dream come true.

CONTENTS

Introduction

Hi! I hope we'll be spending some hours together over the next days and weeks, so I wanted to say *Hello* and introduce myself. You have likely caught my name is Michelle, and I wish I was there in person to hear yours. If I were reading this book, I'd be curled up on my recliner sofa, covered in a thick squishy blanket (it's a thing even though I live in Florida), and there would be a season-related drink to sip while turning the pages. That is how I picture you reading this book as well... although the blanket is definitely an option!

If we had met each other in public – *an event, party, church* – we likely would have started our conversation by saying hello and then asking, "What do you do?" Then we would carry on, talking about our jobs and the type of work we're in. That information somehow seems to define a bit of who we are to each other, doesn't it?

In a sense my career *did* define me, especially in the years after I had become single again. With my failed marriage and the struggle of learning to be single, work felt much easier! Unlike my personal life, work was something I had control over. So I poured myself into my career and I know, to a large degree, it did define me. I like to think, however, that I also defined it!

For the better part of my career, I was a Senior HR Business Partner. I worked in large corporations and had quite the ride dealing with challenging situations in the workplace. The most rewarding part of my career, though, was not in handling the wild scenarios. What I loved most was coaching and developing leaders. I genuinely enjoyed tackling big problems together and encouraging others through the experience. I then took those situations and, using my creativity and humor, turned them into teaching moments through facilitating leadership workshops. That was the all-time *favorite* part of my career. I tried always to bring my authentic self to those workshops and to my job. I liked to say I brought the *human* to Human Resources.

While I no longer work in the mega corporations, I could not be happier than to be right here in these pages where I can bring that same humor, teaching moments, and encouragement to others on a personal level. And who knows, one day this may lead to a speaking invitation for one of your groups! *To which I would gladly accept.*

> So there you have a snippet of my personality and background. While I am rather 'put together' in public, it is my desire always to stay authentic, encourage others, and keep humor in every day of my life!

Through this book, my goal and desire is for you to feel supported and encouraged. I want you to know that, not only have I walked in your shoes, but hundreds (upon hundreds) of others are also walking in them. They, too, are experiencing much the same emotions and challenges. I hear it frequently. Male or female, younger or older, *it is hard to be single.*

In this period of life, it can feel like you are in a void with no boundaries, no timeline, no ground for your feet... and thinking *no one* understands or realizes what your life is like. I once had a conversation with, surprisingly, a younger person who said, "These things just aren't talked about and you think you're the only one!"

That is why I wrote this book. I do not wish for anyone to go through what I went through. Wondering if this is my lot in life. Wondering if I am crazy and might not realize it. Thinking something surely is wrong with me. Convinced I must be unlovable. And every day coming home from work to a quiet, empty house to reinforce those inner thoughts. I am writing of my experiences, echoed in dozens of conversations I've had with others through the years.

These pages are the fulfillment of an idea I had shortly after I became single again. I wanted to write candidly about my experiences and those of so many other singles who have talked with me. I wanted to offer support to those unexpectedly finding themselves alone in this world. To those who have been single way longer than expected. To help all of us know that there are so many others who feel the same way. To let you know these feelings and experiences are normal. They are not necessarily pleasant or good, and they *are* normal. You will have times when you have unrealistic thoughts, bad dates, make poor choices, struggle financially, feel insecure, and be treated differently than when you were partnered. It is not like that every day, but on the bad days, I want you to know we've all had them! You are okay and you are going to be okay.

As others began to confide their experiences to me, I realized there should be a book reassuring everyone that You. Are. Not. Alone. Something to help women adjust to single life after divorce, death, or breakup from a long term relationship. I used to think, *if I can help just one person through my book*, then it will be worth it to know I made one person's life better. However, if I might encourage 10 or 100 or more... I'm certain my heart could not contain that.

This book is our journey together. To be honest, some of the days will be a journey, and others... an adventure. This is not a book where you learn that a handsome form of royalty is going to show up and sweep your heart away by the last page. It is two people (you and me) spending time together talking about the very real, everyday challenges that come with living single again. It is your time to say, "Oh my word, you've had that happen, too? Was that horrendous or what?!" It is your time to see that this single road can get bumpy and that many many others feel jostled, too. These pages are here when you wake up at 3 a.m. with wild thoughts running through your head and even your best friend does not want a call from you.

This book is here to encourage you. It is here, *I am here*, to allow you to be human when maybe you have absolutely no one else in your world with whom you can share just how human this experience is. There is no envelope of pixie dust tucked in the back cover that you can sprinkle to make things better. Chapter 5 does not contain the magic potion to make this go away. What I do hope you find in these pages, though, is camaraderie and encouragement as you navigate your single life.

Realistically, being single is often unexpected, generally unwanted, and it can dramatically throw us off course. So while I have no potions or pixie dust, it is my sincere desire for you to feel more balanced by the time you reach the last page. I hope these chapters help you feel more prepared in your path ahead. If this is all new for you, it is my hope you might learn and be spared from mistakes others of us have fumbled through.

I chose my title intentionally. Navigating does not lift you out of a journey, it guides you through the journey. This is what I hope you find as you turn each page. Words to help you choose good paths. Thoughts to prepare you for those uphill climbs. Stories to make your eyes pop open and take note. Ideas to get you through unexpected detours. True navigation for this journey we call single again.

What to expect through the pages...

Even though single life can have a myriad of random feelings and paths, I have laid out the chapters in what might follow a general progression of experiences. The first chapters are designed to help you process your inner thoughts and the interactions you may have with others. Chapters 6 to 8 focus on pushing forward when it's tough. The next chapters talk about the opposite sex and handling unique situations. Chapters 14 and 15 are my personal gift to you. Ideas to lift your spirits! While I encourage you to wait for those chapters, feel free to jump in and out of Chapter 14 on any given day when you need a little boost. By the time you reach Chapter 16, you will have learned I have an affinity for wordplay. That is our last chapter together and I was excited to discover how my word choice was perfectly designed for the final encouragement I wanted to offer you.

Each chapter concludes with a *Next Steps* page to help you process, grow, and put the chapter ideas into action. I encourage you to take the time to reflect and journal as you go along. Physically writing will have many emotional benefits for you. (Plus, buying a new journal is always a fun experience!) In all my single years, my journals were my lifesavers.

This book is truly created for your encouragement. It is my hope you will see yourself in the pages and know that your thoughts and experiences are normal and *shared* with countless others.

For now, settle in with your favorite drink and comfortable spot. Let's dive into this journey we call *single again...*

1

Do You Hear Voices?

Do you hear them??

Yes, *those* voices! I used to hear them all the time. The loud ones roaring in my head. They weren't exactly audible, and no one around me could hear them. Yet they were definitely there. Speaking clearly, speaking loudly to me. Frequently they would get stuck on replay, especially in the middle of the night. The darkness of night seemed to have a repeat button which routinely jammed, refusing to allow for any decent stretch of sleep. There were voices reminding me how alone I was. Distorting my situation. Firing off soundbites of failures. Snippets of awkward conversations. Each voice validating the crack I'd discovered in my confidence level.

It didn't take long before I realized these voices were one of the hardest challenges I would face living my single life. I have so much about this life I want to share with you. But the voices? *These, we tackle first.* As we clear the voices, we clear our path. And a clear path allows us to navigate a healthier, realistic life. I wish I would have known this when my single years began.

If you had known me, you would not have guessed the invisible struggle I was experiencing. Outwardly, I was confident. Emerging in a career which played to my strengths. You would have seen a vibrant woman involved in projects, growing in positions, even winning a few awards. You would have labeled me as outgoing and completely comfortable in my skin.

Where I had no experience or confidence, though, was interacting as a single person. I wanted to have a partner. I wanted to date. I wanted to look and feel normal again. Or at least look and feel normal in my new single-again skin. I wanted to be adjusted and happy. However, I was simply clumsy living this new life. When least expected, those negative voices would appear, supporting my awkwardness and quoting invisible conversations in my head. Not one of them productive or uplifting.

Do you hear them, too?! Those silent voices which can sound absolutely deafening. For the longest time, I thought I was the only one. Little by little, though, I learned we all have various versions of those self-defeating broken records. Reminding us of yesterday's awkward conversation. Exaggerating our circumstances. Bringing guilt for poor decisions made. Building on hurtful jabs we've heard in the past. Beating us up for falling short. Inflating our situation far beyond the actual reality of it.

> Those voices creep in without invitation and can wreak havoc with our emotions!

It was a couple years into my single-again life when I discovered I was not the only one who had these unwanted voices. One of the churches in our city offered a bible study group created specifically for older single adults. *Singles 35 and Better.* Through those connections, I began to slowly adapt into my new life status. Initially, though, I was still dealing with a big dose of self-comparison. Everyone else seemed to be so well adjusted in their lives. From the way they carried themselves, they looked like they truly had it all together. I assumed they had money from their former spouses; they lived in nice subdivisions and seemed to have fulfilling careers. In my mind, they all had the makings and appearances of single agains who were balanced and adjusted far more than I was at the time.

The more I engaged in personal conversations, however, I soon learned I was not the only one finding my way through this single life. Some had serious challenges with their teens. Several had lost everything financially and were starting over. Others were discouraged because it had been years since they'd been on a date. Simply put, the frustrations, fears, hurts, and voices were taunting most of us in one form or another. They just weren't talked about.

On one occasion, a good friend was talking with me about her commute to work earlier that week. She went on to tell me how she had driven down the highway one morning thinking, "I am soo lonely!" If you knew my friend, you would never guess she would have had those thoughts. She was completely put together!

Our conversation continued as we talked about similar situations we'd been through. I told her I should write a book so others could know they were not alone in what they are experiencing. She, along with many others since, have told me to *please* write the book! I've even had singles younger than 35 say, "I would read that book!"

It has taken some years to get to this place where I can dedicate time to writing. What surprises me though is, all these years later, those who are single again are still feeling lonely. Singles still have voices running in their heads. Telling them no one is out there for them. Voices challenging their decisions. Voices of guilt. Questioning worth. Still convincing. Still isolating.

When it feels like the single-again life is lonely and no one understands, please find comfort in knowing there are numbers of others experiencing the very same thing. Even if they appear more adjusted than you, they have their voices and bad seasons, too. Maybe they've been at this longer with more time to adjust; however, others *are* walking in your shoes. Rest assured, everyone has their moments.

Outrageous Decibels

When I first became single again, the voices in my head were absurdly exaggerated. The problem was, I was not experienced enough and had no one around to tell me those repetitious mantras were embellished. It didn't matter if it was the middle of the night or broad daylight. Whether eating breakfast alone or grabbing a burger in a crowded food court. Sitting in the pew at church or a waiting room at the doctor's office. The voices sounded off. They were sounding off all kinds of statements. I remember they sometimes would loudly announce to the world that I was alone. They told me people could see I wasn't good enough to have a husband or a steady date. They were so compelling, I simply allowed them to speak without even questioning their validity!

Realistically, though, being single did not make me an outcast or a public spectacle. I did not have an ever-present spotlight over my head revealing to everyone I was now single. Looking back, even though my personal community would have known I had divorced, I am positive they did not think more than two thoughts about it. However, during those first months, I allowed the negative voices to control my confidence – and my reality.

I felt truly awkward being single. I had been coupled for decades, so living in a relationship structure was my normal. Now, the other half of my balance was missing. Add to this, I was surrounded by married people in my circles. I felt as though I was sticking out like a sore thumb. I remember being so self-conscious, I even avoided the mall on Friday nights! Why? Because my voices were telling me people would know I was *single*. In my mind, it was a status symbol to have a husband. To be without a husband, then, equated to being not wanted. I was literally too embarrassed to go out in public on Friday nights because I just knew people would be staring at me and they would see I was without a partner.

Let's dissect this rationale... First of all, in my larger city, I did not know a soul who would have been at the mall on a Friday night, so why did I even care what people thought? Secondly, maybe I had a husband at home and I only needed to do some shopping. My thoughts were completely illogical, yet they felt very real and personal. For me, it was embarrassing. It was Friday night, date night, and I did not have a date. (Why did I think Friday was date night anyway?? Nonetheless, I did.) I thought it would appear I was not good enough to have a partner. It was probably more than a decade before I had the courage to go shopping in public on a Friday night. It never occurred to me that not once in my life had I ever noticed a person in the mall and considered them to be unworthy of a date partner! The thought was completely irrational, and yet I allowed that voice to speak fear into me for years and years.

I had a host of other voices firing at me, as well. When we moved to Tennessee, we had chosen a wonderful area because of its good school system. Thus, after I divorced, that location left me alone in a white collar community. I was managing finances with my lower single income, and I did not live in one of the newer subdivisions. Needless to say, the voice of comparison was one which frequently found its replay button in my head. The other women had traveled, and I had barely experienced the world at that point. I didn't have all the local socialite experiences. I just knew men wouldn't find me desirable. – Certainly, I was too vanilla.

I was outgoing in nature, thus getting a date was not extremely difficult. Beyond dinner though, I had zero confidence someone would find me appealing. I even had voices telling me my house was not brick, therefore no man in town would want me! Listen, if a brick house is high on a man's list of desirable qualities? *Run!* Lord have mercy that is so far-fetched. What was I thinking?!

A Lesson in Comparison

Do your voices of comparison wreak havoc on you? Mine were on fire. Until one day, in a random interaction, I learned a lesson which turned everything around. That conversation has stayed with me, and I hope it will have a positive influence on you, too.

I was under new medical insurance and, for the first time, had to go to one of those larger eye care centers located in our mall. This was different for me, so I was taking it all in and meeting the staff for the first time. As I was waiting, I observed the woman who was going to be the one helping me. She was well dressed and wearing the most beautiful diamond ring on her finger!

Because I married young, my wedding ring had been a simple, small solitaire with a thin white-gold band. As I watched the woman helping adjust others' glasses, I started thinking how lucky she was to have a ring so special. How blessed she was to not only have a husband, but to have one who would give her such a gorgeous diamond. Wow. I sat there picturing that experience in my mind.

A few minutes later, my thoughts were interrupted when she was ready to help with my appointment. I'm not sure how our personal conversation began. Most likely, I had complimented her beautiful ring. The next thing I knew I was hearing her story... At some point in their marriage, her husband had a fling with a younger woman who ended up pregnant with her husband's child. The woman continued her story... She and her husband had children already, and their relationship was not horrible, so this situation had not led to divorce.

Now, this woman, who minutes before I had watched with envy, is telling me the sad story of their marriage. She was now coparenting a child, who became her husband's child *while* they were married. She was raising this child in her family alongside their own children. She lived with a constant reminder of the betrayal of the man she loved, as well as a constant connection to the woman who caused it.

From that day, the voice of envy and comparison completely shifted in my way of thinking. If it ever tries to sneak back in, and it rarely does, I quickly remind myself, I don't know what someone's life is like or what hidden challenges they may be living.

That striking interaction was such a turning point for me, and I hope it has an impact on you, as well. How much did those senseless moments of envy gnaw at me? For nothing! We have no idea what is someone's whole story or what invisible battles they may be facing. The voice of comparison is simply defeating and has no redeeming value for us. Not for me. Not for you.

Managing Self-Esteem

There are going to be times when those inner voices will attack your confidence, making you doubt your worth as a partner. Any number of life situations will contribute to those feelings of self-doubt. Maybe you've come from a breakup or divorce (maybe you've come from several) and you caught the brunt of the blame. Or you may be living in a family situation with a fair amount of dysfunction, and you are certain no one will accept your chaotic package deal. Perhaps your self-esteem takes a beating when you look in the mirror at your physical appearance and you feel certain no one will be attracted to what you see in the reflection. Any one of these circumstances, along with so many other scenarios, will stir self-deflating messages, attempting to convince you, you are not wanted and not worthy of love or partnership. *This is untrue!*

When a divorce or serious breakup occurs, there is almost always a history of interactions which happen before the actual event. These interactions simply take a toll on your self-esteem. – An unspoken shift in the relationship, hurtful exchanges, unmet needs, reduced communication, unfaithfulness, etc. If you've come from a relationship where you were constantly badgered, those wounding words will constantly rear up trying to convince you of your shortcomings. Additionally, the buildup is often gradual which can mean months or years of second-guessing yourself, your self-worth, and your value as a partner. When this defeating experience catches up with you, the haunting voices of self-doubt can become overwhelming and they are not so easy to shake.

> **Whether it's from a broken relationship, chaotic family, poor choices, or lack in your appearance, the taunting voices will fire... and they are difficult to hush.**

You may have voices about your relationships. Family. Choices. Appearance. Any one of these situations honestly may be somewhat true in your life right now. But the exaggeration of them?? That is not true! If you are currently experiencing replays of failures or messages reinforcing your lack of worth, please remember these three important truths:

#1 You are not alone. Everyone at some point, in some way, has experienced the very same feelings. They hit the best of us.

#2 It *is* possible to make these voices either go away or go so far it will be hard to hear them!

#3 Regardless of your past mistakes, regardless what your head is telling you, you deserve to be loved and valued.

In the next chapter, we'll look at ways how to keep these negative volumes turned down and restore our self-worth. That process, though, is most effective when we first approach our defeating voices with a solid, realistic mindset. At a time when I truly needed to experience this, I received a piece of encouragement. *It was one simple sentence.* Simple, yet it completely turned my thoughts into a different way of viewing my situation. If you have not had a moment like this, I want to offer you the same encouragement I received...

It was mere months after my divorce. July to November to be exact. I'd married young, so at this point I was living single life truly for the first time. And those internal voices were already in full swing! On that particular Sunday, I was making the drive back to my home state after our family Thanksgiving.

Without warning, I experienced a serious car accident. In a matter of seconds, my young face was damaged severely, leaving me completely unattractive. Heading across the interstate that day at 70 mph, a large buck with a rack of antlers charged my vehicle and lunged through my windshield. As I turned my head for the impact, it broke through the glass and ripped up the majority of the left side of my face. At the time, I was

in my thirties and only four months single again. You can imagine the devastation. How do you start life over when you look like a monster and you know you will have permanent scars?

When the accident occurred, I had only been on the road for an hour, so my family was contacted and able to get to the emergency room to be with me. While I was extremely grateful to be alive, I still had to face the reality that my life had just changed, *dramatically*. I remember lying there with my physical appearance completely destroyed. I looked over to my mom and quietly said, "No one will want to date me now." God bless her, she had the best response ever: "If some man does not want to date you because you have scars, then he is not worthy of you!"

My mother's simple response provided such a turning point for me. It literally set the tone for all future voices that would want to rear up and tell me I was unattractive and undeserving. How unfair, those voices had already begun forming before I'd even left the emergency room! From that moment, though, I knew I would embrace her positive response about my horrible dilemma.

Do I still have scars on my face? Yes, I do. But do they control or belittle me? Not in the least. Hearing those wise words from my mom gave me a whole new perspective I had not considered. I did not need to feel as though I had to "measure up" in my appearance for someone; rather, I needed to find someone who merely fit where I was and where I was heading in life. Someone worthy of me would overlook those scars and see *me*, as a person.

If you don't have anyone in your life acknowledging you, please allow me, right now, to speak these same words into you: If someone does not want you because you have __________, they are not worthy of you! Another way to say this – *They are not the person for you!* The right person will see "you" through your imperfections. All of them.

> **Whether you have physical scars or scars from mistakes, if someone wants to judge you for a lack in your life –**
> ***They are not worthy of you!***

Whether you have made mistakes, need to refine your social skills, have disappointed your family, or let yourself go physically, remember, these moments do not define you. Your voices will try to convince you otherwise. They will taunt you. Tell you it's too late. Belittle you. They'll replay the "if only" in your mind. But remember, they are embellishing and overshadowing the real *you*. You are good. And you are deserving.

Wherever you find the volume level of those debilitating voices, however beat up you may be feeling, please rest assured *everyone*, at some point, has had some degree of these experiences. They might sound different than yours. They may come from different sources. But they are there. Making us feel less than, insecure, inadequate, foolish, unworthy. Regretful. Failed. Alone. They repeat in the dark. They make you feel like you are the only one.

You. Are. Not. Alone. You may be in a rough patch right now, and you will get through this. You have worth. You have a future. These voices happen to the best of us. And I'm here to confirm, there is restoration, there is hope, and there is peace from those voices.

On the following page, the Next Steps exercise will help you sort through which voices are accurate and which ones are merely embellished. Please take some time to pause here and reflect. (Tip: You'll need a pen and paper – and maybe a pack of matches!)

Once you process your thoughts, we'll next work on how you can gain control over those voices rather than letting them have control over you. I'm here rooting for you and I'll see you in a couple pages!

NEXT STEPS

Something to think about...

When are you vulnerable to hearing voices?

Something to move forward...

Acknowledge that your voices are irrational and embellished.

Something to do...

> Write out each of your self-defeating messages. Take a deep look.
> Which ones are embellished? Be realistic!
> Next, label two pages: "Can Work On" and "Exaggerated"
> Rewrite your statements on the pages where they belong.

Acknowledge each page verbally! Yes, Repeat after me....

> Page 1: "I'll work on these as I can. I am human, after all!"
> Page 2: "These are only voices. I am removing them today!"

Now, have a destruction ceremony!
Yes, take Page 2 and BURN it.
Or... Shred... Dispose... Flush.
Oh, flushing will lead to a plumbing bill. Let's not flush.
Whichever you choose, be done with it!
Purpose to move on. You deserve it.

2

YOU

We've all heard the phrase, "Out with old, in with the new!" As I was reflecting on the importance of clearing our negative voices, this phrase came to my mind. And then I thought of it with a fresh twist. Out with the old, *in with the YOU!*

Clearing the exaggerated voices of your past is imperative for you to navigate forward with a healthier balance and a more realistic sense of who you are. *Out with the old.* And then?? Next – *In with the you!* Now it's time to focus on you and your personal self-care.

While the term self-care may conjure up visions of treating yourself to a spa day with a shopping spree to the mall, that is actually a misconception. It is more than a Me Day. (It is also more cost effective and a bit longer lasting!) I'm sure I have spas and shopping mentioned in Chapter 14, but first things first. We're looking here at inner self-care. It will sustain you much longer than that 90-minute massage, and it fits great on a budget.

Hopefully, you've begun to work on removing the negative voices of the past. And now it's time to *refill*. To refill your life with positive things. Positive thoughts, influences, and relationships.

Even if it takes some time, as you work to rid your mind of the negative voices, you will begin to notice a lighter spirit about yourself. You are getting rid of the unnecessary, disruptive, personal clutter. It's like that feeling on those days when you finally get your overcrowded closets cleaned out. You know, when the shelves are cleared and the bins are loaded for donation? That *ahh* feeling. Clean, tidy. The junk is gone! In the same way, after dumping our negative, personal sound bites, our brain and our life begin to experience that same ahh feeling! Fresh, breathable. Light at the end of the tunnel.

As we rid ourselves of old thought patterns, a shift in our mind takes place. Oddly, the process happening on the inside of our brain truly works similarly to our cleaning ventures! Think about those weekends when you've completed a major decluttering project. You step back and marvel at your accomplishment, and you most likely enjoy those bare shelves for a number of days.

Then, something happens with that newfound space, and human nature kicks in. Can you hear yourself? *Oh, I have those items left in the back closet, now I can shift some of them into this cleared spot.* Or... *Good! I can go buy that new item I've been wanting because I have space for it now!* I imagine you know exactly what I'm talking about.

Well, guess what? Our brains fill the empty spaces in our mind much the same way we fill the spaces in our homes. So as you're working to clear the negative thoughts from your life, it's imperative to fill those freshly cleared open spaces with new positive thoughts and activities. If we fail this step, those freshly cleared *shelves of our mind* will begin to clutter right back up with negative items again. Psychologically speaking, thoughts are going to come in and fill up your brain. (It's what our brains do!) Scientifically, however, the negative type thoughts will be the first to creep in due to our brain's natural protective mechanisms. For this reason, it is ever so important to intentionally fill our mind with positive thoughts and activities.

Think of those shelves you just cleared. If you don't replace them with something fresh, new, and attractive, what's going to happen? Yep. The next time you have junk that needs a place to land, that empty shelf is going to be an all too easy target! Toss. Pile. Stuff. Clutter. Before you know it, those shelves will be back to their disarray again. But if they're filled with beautiful items, there will be no space for nasty clutter!

In this same way, our minds have the same re-cluttering potential as our closet shelves! That's the reason we want to build in our minds a solid, healthy, positive core. When the life challenges pop, because they definitely will, our core will be there to help us make the decision to push through and work on overcoming!

Over the next pages, I encourage you to find an idea and run with it. Make it your own. And by all means, make your emotional self-care a priority to keep propelling yourself forward!

I've chosen 5 key areas which can significantly impact our emotions and self-esteem: Mantras (aka self-talk), Influences, Friendships, Professional Help, and mere Determination. It's all too easy to picture self-care as treating yourself to a good spa day. While that is certainly a very pampering thing to do, it's also costly and and it's over within 90 minutes. I don't want 90 minutes of goodness for you, I want a lifestyle of goodness.

Imagine getting those closet shelves cleared... Now, visualize refilling them with a beautiful plant, your favorite books, a citrus candle, a motivational plaque, and a decorative storage basket. You will love your shelf and there will be no more room for junk to accumulate. This is how you care for yourself!

Mantras

Mantras. I use the term loosely, so no, I am not about to suggest you pretzel up in a corner and start chanting to fix your negative soundtracks! I am, however, going to offer something along those lines to help you rewrite your mind's unhealthy scripts into positive scripts.

When I think of someone repeating mantras or positive affirmations, I have two pictures come to mind. One is the pretzel pose and involves humming. The other is an overly confident, super tan salesman. Do you see him? In front of his steamy mirror, white towel around the waist, combing his sleek black hair, repeating, "I am great! I am wonderful! I am successful!" If that's your image of someone repeating mantras or affirmations, let's get this out of your head. (Like, right now.) It is important to replace our negative soundbites with positive ones, however, I am more the type to practice this with a bit of a toned-down approach. – No uncomfortable leg bends or steamy mirror required!

While you may not want to engage in I-am-wonderful mantras, and this practice might sound ridiculously silly to you, I want you to consider this. If you have self-defeating thoughts frequently running through your head, you are already repeating mantras! Should I say this again? If you have self-defeating thoughts frequently running through your head, you are already repeating mantras! They just happen to be destructive, crushing ones.

I used to be incredibly guilty of this without even realizing it. Then, one day I had a very wise person teach me a concept that was quite life changing. Had I not learned it, I know I would have struggled to believe even the most well scripted mantra I might have created. If you fall into this same trap of the mind, I hope you learn from this, too.

We were in her office with a whiteboard on the wall. She took a dry erase marker and drew a line across the whiteboard. At the left side, she hashed off the end and wrote "0". At the right end, she hashed it off and wrote "100." She then, very wisely pointed to it and said to me, "Michelle, you look at yourself as being at either 100 or *zero!* If you're not at 100, you think you are at zero. There is a lot of space in between these two, and the last I checked there was only one person on this earth who lived at the 100 level." She continued, "I'll agree you probably live in this upper end, however, you cannot humanly be at *100* all the time. And when you're not, it is okay to live around the 90's or 80's!"

Wow, this was the first time I had stopped and realized I was truly living my life to these standards. It was the first time I realized I will make mistakes, I will be imperfect. And this is not only okay, it is normal! Failing at something, even making a really huge mistake, does not place me at zero. It does not place you at zero! I... and you... have other qualities and strengths and worth as a person. I will make mistakes. I have an imperfect personality. I will be an imperfect partner. I will be an imperfect employee. I will miss the mark sometimes as a mom.

Goodness, as I write this, I have to acknowledge there are going to be people who will rate me as a subpar author! Ouch, I am not looking forward to that moment, yet I have to say *it is okay*. Everyone is entitled to their opinions and expectations. I have other qualities. I have value. I have worth. Also, I will not be a total fail. If this book helps only one single person, how rewarding is it to know I helped someone in this life?!

Could my negative book reviews cause me to have new voices erupt? Absolutely. I am human, after all. From that point, though, I will have to make a decision. I will decipher what is valid and make a choice to either correct the mishaps – or find a new passion in life! As for the embellished voices? I will list them out. I will select the ones which don't serve me. Then, I most likely will have a farewell party at the fire pit in my backyard! Exaggerated negative voices are not going to serve any productive purpose in my life, and I will want to send them on their way!

> Remember! People make mistakes. People have quirks.
> People have shortcomings. People have failures.
> All of them. All of us.

If you worked through the *Next Steps* exercise in Chapter 1, you exposed your negative voices on paper, acknowledged the exaggeration level of their validity, and gave them a proper farewell party. Good for you! (And I hope you took time to relish in your accomplishment.) As you were completing that exercise, you then possibly discovered there was a small amount of truth in some of your current negative mantras. THIS IS OKAY. There is something important to realize here: Imperfections and a healthy self-worth can coexist! You can be a genuine work-in-progress and deserve to celebrate positive beliefs about yourself at the same time!

That said, I know it can be challenging when those old negative thoughts are trying to re-engage. And *this* is when our new mantra habits will enter the scene. When your mind wants to jump back and exaggerate your past mistakes and character flaws, this is the time when you will take control of the messages rather than allowing the messages to take control of you. It does not matter how you create your new mantras, (affirmations, positive phrases), call them what you will. The important thing is that you do create new positive messages to repeat to yourself.

What were your old mantras telling you? You are too boring? A train wreck? You're not sophisticated enough? Antisocial? Too aggressive? A witch? Unreasonable? Not sexy enough? Too heavy? Unattractive? A financial mess? It is now time to rewrite that script, *literally*.

When you're ready, find a spot of a quiet moment. You'll want to get your pen and paper again – or better yet use sticky notes. We want these to be visible! Next, you will simply write out positive words or phrases you know you need to hear. Writing them down and keeping them visible is key. Research shows that goals written down are many times over more effective than goals merely tucked in our memory. (By the way, if you're really not good at this, suggestions are coming right up.)

Whether you place these in your journal, on stickies, or jot on a favorite note pad, make them easy and visible. One fun place is a note-to-self under your pillow. (*Sweet dreams!*) I often put notes on my monitor so they stay in my line of sight. How about a tuck in your dresser drawer? Do you have a journal you review before you go to sleep at night? Extra bonus: Repeating positivity before you go to sleep will work wonders for a good night's rest!

If this is new or awkward territory for you, I've listed some ideas on the next page to get you started. Even if this is a bit out there for you, give it a try. You might be surprised! Start with writing, reading, and repeating any (or all) of the sample phrases I have listed. Every one of them is either true or easily doable. Or you can use the ideas for creating your own personal phrases. Then, after you've written your mantras, you'll want to... Repeat. Repeat. Repeat.

Take a moment now to read these phrases out loud:

I have worth.

Deep breath in. Hold. Slowly exhale. Repeat.

After all, I am human.

One good thing about me today was ________.

Everyone has their demons.

I am embracing my imperfections.

It's okay to ask for help.

I can do this!

I deserve to be loved and respected.

If it didn't work out, it was not meant to be!

I'll take 5 minutes. Cry. Scream. Be angry. Then move on.

I will grow from this experience and be the better person.

I am fearfully and wonderfully made.

God, give me strength and wisdom to ________.

It's okay that I am slightly a mess. I have other great traits.

To begin, I can start one baby step by ________.

Remember, by physically writing out your positive affirmations, you will put yourself ten times closer to conquering your voices. More than anything, I want you to know you can conquer mistakes, hurts, embarrassing moments, even epic fails and those ridiculous deflating recordings that endlessly wear you down. Fill those shelves of your mind with positive thoughts. Once you do, there will be no space left for the old thoughts to return. There are good days and successes ahead. This period in time does not define you. Regardless of your situation, you are capable and deserving of a do-over!

Influences

Have you ever taken a pause to consider the influences impacting your life? I have a friend who is loads of fun, but ohh they are a bad influence on my waistline! We never lack for a reason to celebrate or try some yummy dessert. The bottom line is, if I wanted to be skinny as a bean pole, I would seriously need to consider if that person was the best one to hang out with. (Thank goodness I don't need to feel *that* skinny, so all is well!)

The people influences in our lives, are rather easy to spot. You know someone who is constantly negative or complaining, and you want to be more positive? You'll find ways to distance yourself! You've likely had that experience at some point and know what I'm talking about.

In our modern culture of *social media*, however, we are bombarded constantly with influences we may not realize. We do seem to realize the social media influence when it comes to our kids, but do we consider that we are being influenced just as well?! With us though, it may be not so obvious.

We see others posting family events, trips, smiles, beautiful children, remodeled kitchens, you name it. And here we sit, no longer a family unit, budget disrupted, remodels out of the question, and vacations on hold. Next enters your voices of frustration, comparison, envy, etc. Quite frankly, it can be depressing and it doesn't take long for those old thoughts to creep back in. They will clutter and take back over your thought patterns if you're not careful.

If you are struggling with voices of comparison or these posts cause you to feel defeated, your self-care action may be to take a social media break! Consider the impact from viewing Instagram, Facebook, TikTok, etc. You know people are using their pics where the lighting and angles were just right. And while it's natural to want to share a fun trip, a child's accomplishment, or special gifts, we have to remember, these are only snippets of a person's life. Memorable *moments* being shared.

If seeing others' posts is causing you envy, sadness, or it's nipping at your self-esteem, consider taking a time away or turning off certain notifications. When you are feeling better, you can always turn them back on! I have to admit, I have gone through spells where my budget was a bit tight and it can sting to see friends posting their excursions while knowing travel was out of reach for me at the time. The ridiculous thing, I was perfectly content with my life! Without seeing those events, I would have had nothing telling me I was missing out. If your social media is amplifying your defeating messages, it may be time to find your settings button and make some edits. Remember, you are working to create a healthier you.

> Removing a hurtful influence is definitely a step in the right direction!

If you do take a social media break, remember to fill the newly cleared space in your life with something positive! Since we are working on self-care, you might consider downloading a wellness app. I use one for sleep and it has other resources, too. There are sections of daily motivations, relaxing music, and even stretching! Also, your company may have resources available through an Employee Assistance Program. In the past, my company's EAP had a fun event where I completed a Steps Challenge with other participants. I was still involved socially, and it had a healthy purpose!

For another positive online influence, try daily messages from an inspirational app. Or, if you miss social interaction, games often offer the ability to compete with others. I know for me, whenever I clear one area of my routine, I feel a little lost with the new empty space. This is normal and it's okay to fill it back up. Just make sure you're filling back up with positive influences that give you strength, confidence, and support to your overall plan for self-care!

Friendships

When we become single again, the shift in partnership often causes a change in social life with our friends. In a few chapters we'll talk about that more in depth. For now, though, I want to chat about the importance of finding like-minded friendships as it relates to your self-care. Surrounding yourself with understanding people who have walked in your shoes is a positive step in creating a healthy supportive network.

Before I go further, I want to acknowledge that I understand it might feel odd right now to think about seeking friendships with other singles. Depending on how long you were married, if this is all still fresh, you may not yet be at the place where you even consider yourself as *single*. It's not likely a label you asked for, wanted, or want to be called. Please know those feelings are understandable and you are not alone! This transition can feel (and sound) awkward, and I experienced it, too.

Labeling myself as *single* or *divorced* was something that bothered me for the longest time. Honestly, I even disliked filling out forms at the doctor's office. Why did they need to know I was divorced? Nonetheless, it felt like I was confirming failure every time I had to check that box. On the other hand, I really didn't consider myself a completely single person, either. I wasn't twenty-two and fresh out of college. After all, isn't that what they mean by single? And truthfully, I wasn't exactly *single*, I was divorced. It's funny how that little box caused such an emotional experience for me. But it did. It confirmed I was in a new status. My life was different now. I was no longer coupled. I was doing life alone.

Whichever way it is you have come to be no longer married, no longer in partnership, it takes time to adapt to your new status. The idea then of making friends with other singles may be the furthest thing from your mind... or your desires... or your comfort zone! I completely get it. However, finding new friendships will be one of the best things you can do for your *self*. Interacting with others walking in your shoes and handling similar struggles will be a great source of support.

Depending on the size of your community, you may discover different singles groups you might join. Even if singles groups are limited, you should be able to find a church offering Divorce Care or a widows' support group. The important thing to keep in mind is that, by finding others walking in your shoes, you are taking a solid step toward your self-care. Sitting at home alone is going to offer a lot of empty space, and empty space is where that clutter will want to creep back in. Your friendships will be there to lift you up, make you laugh, allow you to vent, and keep you going in the tough times.

Another suggestion, which I understand may fall outside your comfort zone, is to find a church that offers a small group or bible study for older singles. I know it's tough to leave your familiar place. It is awkward to walk into a new church where you know absolutely no one; however, the support and new friendships you form will be invaluable. The more time you spend with others who are walking in your shoes, the more balanced you will feel. You will make friends who understand your life situation and you, in turn, will understand theirs! Those mutual friendships will be some of the best self-care you can give yourself. You will be accepted as you are, and they will be grateful for your genuine friendship, as well.

Professional Help

Leverage a Life Coach.

If you're feeling not quite ready to meet new friends or struggling in adapting to living alone, a Life Coach may be a great option and support for you. If this is an unfamiliar concept, Life Coaches are certified professionals who can help you process your adjustment into this new life status. They'll work with you to reach a more balanced view of your situation, build confidence, and conquer the challenges you're facing. They'll help you set new goals as you work toward creating healthier self-care habits. You can find someone with a basic search of "Life Coaches for Singles" in your area. Remember, as with any new professional, check out their website to get a sense for who they are. Then interview them to make sure they're a match for your style and personal goals!

Note: If you don't get a sense they would be a good fit for you, it's okay to move along. If that feels awkward, just let them know you're speaking with others to find the best fit for yourself and you'll get back with them. I don't generally encourage little white lies, but that's much nicer than saying, "Yehhh, this is *not* gonna work!"

Seek Counseling.

If you sense you are slipping too much with your self-esteem or have bouts of sadness to a point where it is impacting your daily life, please consider seeking someone for counseling. You could be suffering from situational depression and might benefit from a professional to help you through the adjustment period. Depending on your work benefits, you may have options through your company's Employee Assistance Program which are private and often free. Additionally, you may find help through the pastoral staff at your church. These resources can help you either regain your footing or determine if additional support might be helpful. Slipping into a level of depression after death or divorce is very possible, and the right support will help you feel like yourself again!

Determination

In the year I was writing this book, I was facing the unwelcome results of poor eating and exercise habits. For the longest time in my life, I had eaten relatively healthy and stayed active, so these new extra pounds were quite frustrating to me. One day, I'd had enough of the frustration and experienced that freeing moment where I nailed down my decision to go back to my healthier habits and lose the weight I'd gained. And I did! I bought a journal to track my goals and progress, got rid of the bad food in my cupboards, and learned how to use the fitness options on my sports watch. It took only days for me to begin to see the results. Week after week, month after month, I stayed disciplined reviewing my commitment daily and reaping the rewards. Even through traveling, events, and holidays, I stayed disciplined.

Then, 25 pounds down and 7 months later, I found a can of pumpkin tucked back in the pantry. What is worse, I also found the can of evaporated milk to go with it! By this time, autumn was beginning and I longed for that back home feeling you get from old-fashioned, homemade pumpkin pie. In spite of measuring the carbs and attempting to eat healthy proportions, I caved and I won't tell you how quickly I polished off that pie. If that was not bad enough, the same week, my neighbor insisted on doing a kind gesture and brought over food from a local BBQ. I don't need to tell you the result. Where I had been only 2.5 pounds from reaching my overall goal, those bad choices caused me rather to GAIN 2.5 pounds. If you're good at math, it will take you about 3 seconds to realize I was then 5 pounds away from my goal. I was so close, happy with how my clothes were fitting, so proud and excited. And in days I was feeling defeated, sloppy, frustrated. A total failure. In just days, my goal seemed far away. Unattainable.

That morning when I got on the scales, I really wanted to give up. I didn't want to go out and walk my mile. I didn't want to jog the inclines. I wanted to sulk and say, *This is impossible!! I can't do this. It's not worth it. I'll never be able to get back to my goal.*

I know that might sound absolutely absurd. After 7 months and 25 pounds, *why* would I think I now couldn't do it over a simple two pound gain?! – Because those voices were telling me I couldn't! I started to let them control me rather than me control them.

As I write this, I'm not sure what the scales will read tomorrow. But today, I walked my mile. I ate my low carbs. And I recorded in my journal. Even though I don't feel like it, I know there are certain practices which will produce the results I want. Even though my voices are trying to sabotage my self-care, telling me I can't, telling me I don't want to anymore, I know that I *can!*

I experienced today what I am about to ask you to do. When you feel like you've blown it. When it seems hopeless. When you know what's best and you'd rather sit in your sad situation. Join me. Get up out of your slump. Pick yourself up by the bootstraps. I know sometimes it's more comfortable to remain in the slump. It is what we know and, as bad as that might be, it's the easier way.

However, if I go back to my old eating habits. If I stop walking my mile every day. I will gain the weight back. I will be even more disappointed. My clothes will go back to looking tight and my face will round out again. I won't be happy. I won't be healthy. I won't feel good about myself. The voices will win and I will live defeated.

It's hard to change and be intentional with our thought patterns. I'm living that as I type! I do though, want to get back to my successes. I want to feel accomplished again. That means, I have to say *No!* to those voices. And then I have to take the next step and choose healthy. I have to fill my life with the positive. I need to write my positive mantras and keep them visible. I need to leverage my wellness apps, stay away from comparison, and find supportive friends to join me. I have to be willing to do what I'm asking you to do.

Will you step out with me? Determine to keep your commitment of not allowing those defeating messages to return. Take care of yourself. Make YOU a priority. Remind yourself that you can feel balanced and strong again. Even if it doesn't seem like it right now. Even if some of these activities are *far* outside your comfort zone. Let's take at least one step toward our goal of being healthy. I know healthy patterns mean a healthy balanced life, physically *and* emotionally. I'm willing to say no to those horrible voices that tried to creep back inside my head today. I'm willing to take the positive steps I need to feel confident again. Are you? We can do this *together*.

NEXT STEPS

Something to think about...

We all have triggers that will sneak in to sabotage our personal self-care. Where's your weak spot? What puts you in a tailspin?

Something to move forward...

Think about the area of your single life that most needs a confidence boost. Is it improving your self-talk? Changing social media habits? Finding single friends? Asking for help? Staying disciplined?

Something to do...

List one obstacle preventing you from the self-care step you deserve. *What's holding you back?* Create a SMART goal to overcome it!

Specific, **M**easurable, **A**chievable, **R**elevant, and **T**ime-bound.
TIP: Find an accountability partner who will hold you to it!

With pen in hand, write positive personal mantras.
Place visibly. Repeat daily.

3

The Definition of Void

/void/

adjective

– completely empty.

noun

– a completely empty space.

my personal definition

– silence.

– emptiness.

– restlessness.

– boredom.

– quiet.

– blank.

– alone.

– endless.

Even when we begin to have control on our defeating voices or we've created a solid routine of self-care, there is another space of single life which can easily absorb us when it is not approached proactively. And that is *space* itself.

Coming home to an empty house at night. Waking up with no one to share a good morning. Celebrating a personal success... by yourself. Eating in silence. Mindlessly flipping through channels because there is nothing to watch and nothing to do. Walking around a still house with zero motivation for any type of productive activity. Having absolutely no one to talk to. Having no idea when or *if* this lifestyle will ever end. Wondering if this is your lot in life. Living in quiet space with no partner. This is the void which can so easily become our life. If you experience moments (or days) like this, the emptiness is real!

Years ago when email was new, the computer system used to announce incoming messages. (Do you remember that?) During this period, I had a spell where I was between companies and spent much of my time job searching, sitting at the computer in silence. All my peers were at their places of work and I had no partner, so I spent the bulk of my days *and weeks* with hardly any conversation. I remember one afternoon, sitting in complete silence. All of a sudden I had an email come through. Without warning, my computer loudly announced, "You've Got Mail!" Immediately I perked up, looked down at my poodle, and said, "Oh! I had someone talk to me!!"

If you can relate to my story, you likely understand what it is to feel you are living in an endless void. The silence can be deafening. Yet it's not only the silence. The boredom, ahh the boredom. You flip on the TV to fill the space. There is either nothing entertaining or there is not a story line you haven't seen a hundred times already. You look around and glimpse the laundry pile. As necessary as it may be, it holds little intrigue, as do the dishes piling in your sink. It's a hard pass on the chores right now. You make a good decision to walk outside to check the mailbox, enjoy the stretch and two minutes of fresh air, toss the advertisements… and then stare at the walls considering your next mindless activity. This is one definition of void and, as dreadful as it sounds, this pointless routine can easily become your single life. The world of communication you once had is gone and, although we joke about it, *walls really do not talk*.

If your friends or family members have not lived this life, or have not lived it in awhile, they will struggle relating to how empty everyday life gets when you are going it alone. When my mom was living, I used to call her every Monday night. I lived several states away so there was always catching up to do, and sometimes we spent at least an hour talking. It was also nice to merely have conversation outside of work. On one of those call nights, my dad poked at me chiding about what a chatterbox I was. What he didn't realize though, was that I was not a chatter box at all. In reality, I hardly talked. For the seven days prior to that call, outside of work, I had barely uttered a word. What he didn't realize was that he had opportunity to talk with someone throughout his days and evenings whenever he wanted.

My dad didn't realize that every single morning I woke up to the alarm in a silent empty house. I got ready for work in silence and ate breakfast alone in my car on the way to work because there was no one to share my breakfast or my morning. He didn't think about the end of my work day when I had no one to call to simply say, "I'm headed home!" Or that I pulled in the garage every night to a dark, empty, silent house. My dad couldn't picture me cooking dinner in the kitchen by myself without talking because there was no one with whom to talk. He didn't see me smelling the delicious concoction I would create yet having no one to share my accomplishment. He never saw the fun I had trying to plate my creation like the cooking shows... only for myself to enjoy. He couldn't have known what it was like to take my dinner into the living room with the TV because sitting in the dining room alone would be just plain boring. Or that I would eat without talking because there was no one to share my day. He wouldn't have realized I was watching funny shows and laughing with myself on the sofa because there was no one beside me to enjoy the humor. My dad didn't see every single night of my life when it would get late and I would turn off the TV and walk to my bedroom in silence. Brush my teeth and wash my face in silence. Throw on my pajamas and plan my next workday in silence. Then hop into bed in silence. My dad didn't realize that every single morning I woke up to the alarm in a silent empty house...

I wouldn't have labeled me a chatterbox, although I have to admit I did talk to myself a bit!

For those with children at home, it may seem like there is little time for any type of void to settle in. Yet, while there is someone with whom to speak verbally, it is likely those conversations are focused on their lives and school, or their homework, or the woes of young friendships. If television is watched, it is a child's program. Dinner is likely cooked alone and I'm guessing there is not a great appreciation shown for your culinary skills. The activity of family will absorb some of the void... and then the bedroom door is shut, the lights go out, and there it is. The day is over and there was no one with whom to vent about that incident at work or to share the glowing compliment received. And no one to wrap their arms. So we go to sleep, wake in the morning, and begin the routine. Again.

Whether you are home with just yourself or at home handling a family, living life without a partner can sometimes feel vast and vacant. Lonely. Lacking. Off. Sometimes it is unsettling. And sometimes you wonder if it will ever go away.

Let me confirm, these feelings are real and you will think the only way to get through this is to give up. (What does that mean anyway??) I know it might feel extremely unpleasant right now. It might not be your time to have a partner. It might be some years down the road. But, give up? No. Perhaps shift your thoughts about it? Yes. Let's focus on merely shifting your thoughts rather than throwing them completely out the window. This way is healthy, more balanced, and allows you to approach the void with a much more positive attitude.

Balance in the Void

Before I begin these next thoughts, I want to be clear about my perspective on *living* in the void. I hope to encourage you with ideas that will help you keep your balance when the waves of emptiness come in and refuse to leave. The reality is, you will experience days when those invisible waves seem to hit harder than others. When those days or moments arrive, it is completely acceptable to take your time to grieve, to be angry, to take a spell of sadness, and even spend some much-deserved time to sulk and feel sorry for yourself. I don't believe it's good to live in denial or merely cover our feelings pretending they are not there.

That said, I know those moods are sometimes the easier place to remain; they are natural and definitely the path of least resistance for our emotions. I can certainly slip into my frustrated-angry-sulking mode with almost zero effort! I know it might feel comforting to curl up with a bowl of your favorite ice cream and just stay there. It's easy and you deserve to have your moment. However, living in this spiral, is truly not a healthy place to reside for long. You cannot sustain a balanced life if you live consistently in this space.

If you are reading here while currently inhabiting one of those slumping voids, keep eating your ice cream! I made a commitment to myself (and you) about the intent of this book. This is not a read where I tell you how you're going to snap out of it and instantly be happy living the single life. To put it frankly, some of us simply *don't like* being single and we *want* to be married or at least in a relationship. Even if you're not ready for a relationship right now, you still may not consider it fun living alone. For those of us who fit these categories, all the happiness advice in the world will not fully replace the emptiness of living life without a partner.

Is the answer to merely live in sadness then? Absolutely not. But there is balance! Creating a focus on balance is realistic, attainable, and it is healthy. It's good for you, and it's good for those around you.

> My hope is to help you feel encouraged *in* the disappointment and emptiness.

Over these next pages, I'm happy to share realistic ideas on how you can easily pull yourself up to make your life better. I've learned ways to neutralize the stir-crazy times; those days when you wonder if there is any end to this loneliness or this lifestyle. When I learned these, I finally began to experience more peace. With that peace, my contentment rose and the void settled.

I learned that I can focus on having a fulfilling life for myself at the same time I may be grieving the loss of relationship or acknowledging I was done wrong. It's about thinking differently *for yourself*. It's allowing *you* to have control over your situation, rather than allowing it to have control over you. It's about finding a balance. As we learn to balance the everyday void of living alone, our emotions will begin to level, and life will begin to develop new meaning in different ways.

A Lifesaver Concept!

Along my journeys (*I've had lots of them*), I met a life coach who taught me a concept about time frames which I had never heard before. Up to that point in my life, when I wasn't around people at work, I really did not enjoy the free space of living alone. Looking back, I'm fairly certain I worked long hours simply to avoid the emptiness. (That's not a good habit, by the way!) One day, in conversation with this coach, we were talking about the void of being single, and she taught me about planning out the blocks of time in my day. This was a major breakthrough point for me and quite the lifeboat for floating in the void. Here's how it works:

In our personal everyday life, it is beneficial to think of our waking hours as having three core time blocks. Not surprising: morning, midday, and evening.

The Morning Blocks. Think of a Saturday, or your specific day off work. Have you ever found your mornings aren't so empty? You're busy making the bed, maybe exercising, catching a shower, picking an outfit, and grabbing breakfast. That's your morning block and you likely don't feel so much of a void because it is filled with your set routine. Then the routine ends. And what now?

This is where planning out our time blocks is beneficial. If you have a plan created, it helps to fill your void, give you structure, and it provides something to look forward to. Thus, it minimizes the empty feeling of being alone. Left unplanned, when we roll past that morning block, the afternoon and evening blocks in our day can easily become ever so quiet and lonely.

So how does this work? How do I fill up my time blocks? Are we talking about planning a day trip to a nearby city? Making reservations for a fancy dinner with a friend? Well, maybe down the road; however, that's not what I had in mind. For any of the blocks, it is not so much *what* you plan, rather it is *that* you plan! I recommend doing this at least a few days before your free time so you can be prepared. I also highly recommend writing it on your calendar. (Yes, I used the word *writing*. One of my favorite old fashioned things in life is my kitchen calendar hanging by the back door. The visual keeps me balanced and on track!)

The Midday Blocks. Let's specifically look at the midday blocks for the times you consider your days off work. I'm guessing for most of us, this is where the void might first rear its ugly head. Note, this planning is not so much about creating some phenomenal outing, although that is a smashing idea when you're ready!

> It's about creating structure for yourself, a focal point, with purpose.

If you've worked all week, your day-off midday plan may very well be laundry, cleaning the bathrooms, or checking your budget. If you have kids, it might be a trip to the mall for those new shoes. In the summer, yard work is likely top of the list. Whether it's for necessities or a much desired walk at the park, having a plan is the key here. The plan allows your mind to go from morning routine to, "Ah, this is next on my to-do's!" Do you see how that happens? There is no *void* because there is no void. There is no empty space for meandering thoughts, boredom, sadness, or anger.

The midday blocks may be fairly easy to plan. There is always going to be cleaning, shopping, groceries, and appointments. The benefit of writing them down in advance is that it minimizes the chance of indecisive thoughts arising and our minds stewing over what we should do... which in turn magnifies our aloneness. It provides a direction to point your body after you've finished breakfast. A compass of sorts. If you are following a compass, then you are headed somewhere and not meandering in a void wilderness.

The Evening Blocks. These may feel like the most challenging time spaces as a single person. And they also might be the most fun to plan! I didn't say evening blocks were the most fun, they simply might just be the most fun to *plan*. I personally believe evening time exaggerates emptiness and the void of being alone. This was the time of day when, in the past, my thoughts would run wild reminding me that I was home alone and had no one to be with. Planning out evening time blocks allowed my focus to shift toward the activity I set for myself. It allowed my attention to draw toward something *good* rather than dwell in my situation of being alone.

One thing to remember is you are designing these time blocks to keep yourself balanced in your thought life. This is not about starting elaborate hobbies or planning expensive outings with friends. It's about thinking which evenings this week you are going to be free and what activity you can plan in advance so the emptiness does not catch you off guard and throw you into a tailspin! If you have the opportunity to plan dinner with a friend, by all means, take advantage. Realistically, I know that is not always an option. There are times when schedules or budget simply do not cooperate with desire. When those times hit, there are other easy things you can do to keep yourself occupied. Below are some of the ways I've filled my empty space. Feel free to snag an idea to create your own moments and traditions!

Time Block Ideas

The first idea is probably fairly basic and one I'm sure you have on your checklist. Nonetheless, this is how I make it my own. Please enter the "no judgment zone" here. I have a bit of a musical background, so I really enjoy some of the competition shows like AGT, Idol, and Dancing with the Stars. I even make sure I vote for the best talent. This gives me a little extra purpose and something to look forward to each week during the competitions. To top it off, I'll pop a bag of popcorn and curl up to enjoy the whole experience!

I also used to watch the Bachelor seasons. As I got older, I did take a break for a while and then oddly started watching again. In the beginning I had created a tradition for myself and, even though that was some years ago, I still keep it. For the finale, I order a pizza and have my own watch party night. Even though it might sound silly, these simple shows and traditions have given me something to do and look forward to. They've kept my mind focused on lighthearted fun and have filled the void that might otherwise creep in during the night hours.

To provide variety beyond the TV, I enjoy treating myself to a new novel or jigsaw puzzle. While either of these could be purchased online, actually *shopping* for them is an event in itself. It gets you out of the house and allows you to spend time in a different environment. So freshen yourself up, put on something that makes you feel good, splash a little lipstick, and take a trip into town! While you're there, say hello to someone. It will feel good on you! And who knows, you may make a new friend in the process. At the least, your smile will help someone else feel a little less lonely.

Even if your time is limited for working puzzles or reading novels, either of these two activities have no issue waiting on you between available nights. Additionally, these hobbies are not for any certain age group. To my surprise, I have run across young people of all ages, from 20's to 40's, guys and gals, who enjoy both reading and jigsaws! These are both amazing ways to get your mind focused on something besides yourself.

Another filler activity might be to try a new recipe. It's fun, time consuming, and requires your full attention. Again, minimizing space in the void. An added bonus, if you make a new snack, it could double as your personal party food for one of your shows! I did this just the other night. I was really hungry and completely forgot how long it took zucchini lasagna to bake. (*Ugh*) So I took a bit of the leftover ingredients and made myself some hors d'oeuvres. I put white cheese slices on club crackers, sprinkled with Italian seasoning, placed small pieces of my lasagna beef, topped with spaghetti sauce, dusted parmesan, and microwaved just 'til melted. Then I arranged them on a nice plate, poured a drink, lit a candle, and spoiled myself with a delicious pre-dinner appetizer! Not only was this practical, it was ridiculously easy, entertaining, and gave me a special treat-to-self.

By the way, I'm looking forward to us arriving at Chapters 14 & 15. I reached my goal to come up with 101 ways to treat yourself. They are great time block ideas!

Are all of these things more fun with another person? Yes, certainly, they are! The reality? I don't always have another person around. However, simply because I'm alone does not mean I have to sit at home feeling sad or sorry for myself. Besides, I can always snap a pic of my fun and send it to my kids or a friend. And although these activities do not replace having a partner with me, they *do* help fill the void and allow me to focus on something positive!

Beware! The Void. No Boundaries.

While the practice of planning time blocks is great for curbing those daily lulls of emptiness, it is healthy to understand and accept there will be other seasons of void that hit when you least expect them. These voids are not always time sensitive! I have had lengthy spells where I felt as though I was *living* in the void. Not happy at all about being single. Realizing it had been year over year and I was nowhere closer to finding a partner, much less a *life* partner. I truly hated going through the motions day in and day out all by myself.

When these seasons come, please know they are normal and you are not alone. They happen and they are not fun. If I may be so blunt, sometimes they are downright horrible and they can take you down the path of feeling hopeless. When you fall into one of these lulls that want to suck you in and keep you discouraged, as I've mentioned, I am a firm believer in allowing yourself the freedom to experience your emotions. It is healthy to acknowledge your sadness, hurt, frustration, anger, your emptiness. It is staring you in the face, so there is no need to deny what you're feeling!

However, the time of sulking *has* to have boundaries! Take 5 minutes behind closed doors or 5 hours one afternoon at the park. In whatever way it fits your schedule, give yourself permission to get it out. Then, once you've had your honest, bold, verbal expression, pick yourself up and wipe your eyes. You *have* to do this. Staying down and defeated will do you no good, nor will it be good for your family, your friends, your neighbors, or the strangers you pass along the way. Have you ever seen a sour person at the grocery store? It is no fun to pass by someone like that. They pull you down and produce negative, *wasted* attention. You really do not want to be that person. It is okay to acknowledge your frustration. It is not okay to allow that frustration to control your life.

God Talked!

Sometimes these seasons come in so strongly, it can be overwhelming. I have experienced relationship after relationship not working out. I have experienced having no one in my circles even close to compatible to my life. I have even seriously considered that I must simply be an *unlovable* person and thus destined to be alone. (This is not true, by the way, yet I had gone to the place I was convinced it was truth.) For me personally, these are the times I dig deep and fully rely on God to bring me through.

When I remember and acknowledge that my life is fully in God's hands, I am able to step outside myself and trust there is a greater purpose for my life. A few years back I was feeling a bit overwhelmed with one of these trials. As I was praying (aka complaining) to God about it one day, it was almost as if I heard Him speak out loud back to me. And do you know what He said?

...Michelle, sometimes it's not always about you.

Ohh, ouch. That stung. ('You see why I think God said it? I don't seriously think I would give myself that message.) Nonetheless, it was stated, and it completely changed my focus... and my complaining... and the overall outlook on my circumstances.

That simple yet stunning sentence, "*It's not always about you,*" stopped me in my tracks. I wanted to be selfish. I wanted to wallow in my self-pity. I wanted my life to be different. You notice there's a whole lot of "I" in there. However, when did life exactly become all about me?? Of course I would like my life to be good and happy. Yet why do I think my life would be *unhappy* if it were focused on others or a greater purpose God has for my life? The reality is, my peace, won't come from having a husband or special job or a certain house. My joy is not in things. It's in my life with God and *His* purpose.

I have since accepted that life is not always about me, sometimes it's about the other person. Maybe I am put in this situation so that I might bless someone else. It might feel like it hurts too much or I'm scared or it's hard on me but, *it's not always about me.* It might be about **you**. God might need to use me to help you. I am His vessel, His instrument.

> When I realize that, I am okay with my situation.
> I am no longer in a void – I am in a *purpose*.

NEXT STEPS

Something to think about...

Do you have a sense you are off-kilter? Struggling to feel complete? Give yourself permission to be okay with that.

Something to move forward...

How is your void impacting you and others around you? Could you specifically make a commitment to begin thinking differently?

Something to do...

Start a new hobby, or plan one time block activity, as your first step in creating a fulfilling new approach to life.

Sometimes it's not always about us.

4

Opinions...

Opinions... Everybody's got one!

As you journey through your single life, whether you have recently become single again or you have been here awhile, you will undoubtedly bump into others' opinions along the way. It could happen as your new life is beginning to take shape. Or opinions may pop during a time you decide to make personal changes. For any number of reasons through this journey, you will make decisions for yourself on how best to move forward. Even when you are confident your changes are positive and healthy, others may have completely different ideas what is best for you. Not that it's their business, mind you, but they will have them! Good, bad, or otherwise. People will form opinions and you will quite possibly hear about them.

Buckle up. If you haven't experienced this yet, others' opinions can swing into your lane when you least expect them! And some of them can sting. And some of them will come from people who have not walked in your shoes. This is not to say they are given with malice. Many people think they are helping. Some think they are bringing humor. Some are merely judgmental.

If you are widowed, you may hear opinions genuinely given out of ignorance regarding the depth of your loss or your situation. If you are single from divorce or breakup, you might have experienced negative opinions before your single status even began. Well-meaning or hurtful, the opinions of others can be overwhelming.

In whatever way we hear them, opinions can catch us off guard. Sometimes we fall for them, absorbing them as truth. They can grow in our minds and wreak havoc on our self-esteem. They can cause us to second-guess our judgment. Simply put, opinions can hurt.

Years ago I learned a lesson from a co-worker and have tried to embrace this mindset ever since. One day she told me about receiving some fairly negative feedback at work and I asked, "Didn't that bother you?" Her response: "No! You know what they say about opinions... *everybody's got one!*"

You've likely heard that saying (along with the extra line), but for me it was a first. In our single lives, more than ever, we need to keep that attitude tucked in close. If someone has not walked in your shoes (and no one has exactly), they have no right to judge. And we have no obligation to receive their judgment!

Handling Past Opinions

As I was envisioning the idea to cover this topic of opinions with you, my thoughts initially went toward those types of opinions we hear *after* we become single again. And then a peculiar thing happened. In speaking with other singles I began to see that many of us, male and female, are being impacted also from *past* opinions. They've come from our marriages. Unhealthy relationships. From people we looked up to. I began to see these judgments are just as impacting, if not even more so, than the ones we receive today.

If you repeatedly heard negative comments about yourself, they have likely stuck with you and, to a degree, may still define you. Those opinions will have an impact on your current single life and are the ones we want to address first. Freeing yourself from the impact of the past will allow you to proceed with confidence and balance in your future.

Have you had someone take the liberty to speak their opinions at you? Even in jest, you may have absorbed them enough to believe they are true. But have you ever stopped to think... *Where did these come from?* Who did they come from? Are they truly valid?? Even if there was some validity, does that person's perspective define you? It's time to take those statements that have inaccurately molded you and be rid of them.

Have you heard of the five love languages? As you might guess, one of my languages is *Words of Affirmation.* You can imagine how words can get absorbed into the creases of my brain and have such an influence over me. I remember one day not long after my divorce, I was driving up the road and thinking about my negative personality traits. Those thoughts were on a roll that afternoon as my brain fired off things I'd heard in the past.

Suddenly, the strangest realization occurred to me. These negative thoughts had come from my marriage. And before I go any further, let me explain! My ex-husband and I get along extremely well. He's great. We merely married young and had two different personalities. In that marriage, then, you can guess there was some poking that happened. Even though the pokes were said jokingly, my mind exaggerated them as confirmation that I had a few difficult traits. (I admit I can be challenging, but *not* to the level my internal voices were firing.) Here's how this works: Teasing words + partial truth + raging internal voices = Opinion blown out of proportion! Have you had this happen? – *Time to dissect another rationale!*

As I was driving up that road, a reality hit me. Those traits which my mind had grown into gospel truth, were opinions (albeit teasing) from our early marriage. We were inexperienced *teenagers*. For two decades I had let the opinion of a teenager influence who I thought myself to be! That is incredibly irrational. My mind, though, was so wrapped up in believing the opinions, I had never thought to break away to consider the validity or my own self-exaggeration of them.

Then, something rather amazing happened, which completely shifted my self-perception. I was so struck by the thought that I had allowed a very young guy to influence my self-image, I decided to nail this experience of revelation once and for all! I took out a spiral notepad. (Yes, I was still driving up the road and had paper with me. I do not recommend this exercise while driving; however, I do highly recommend the exercise! It was such a moment.) I took out that notepad. I can still see it partly covering the steering wheel and my lap. I can still see the trees and hillsides of Franklin Road. Still see the gray interior of my vehicle. I took out a pen, ferociously ready to make my list. I was going to write EVERY negative word, every trait I had ever been labeled when we were young. I was going to make this list and tell those words they were the opinions of a teenager and I did not have to accept them anymore! They were not accurate and I didn't have to live by those opinions any longer! *I was fierce.*

So I took that pen and I wrote... one phrase. One phrase. I wish I could remember now exactly what I wrote. (Isn't that funny? I remember everything about that life-changing moment, except for the exact phrase I wrote on that paper.) Then, much to my surprise, as I tried to write other words, there really weren't any other words. As I looked at that paper, I realized for all those years I allowed one opinion to grow in my mind causing me to feel *flawed*. I had allowed one small thought to grow large enough to overshadow and incorrectly mold so many areas of my self-perception. But in the end, the reality is, my personality was merely *different* than my young husband's personality. It did not make me a lesser person; it merely made me different. And that day, driving up that road, I put away my exaggerated, overblown, defeating self-opinion. I nailed the lid on it and, for the first time in decades, came to embrace *me* for who I am.

Have you heard opinions that have impacted you over the years? What words have inaccurately molded you? What have you believed because someone said them to you? Do you have negative words labeling you because someone told you that is who you are?

Is it time to take out a spiral notebook and pen to ferociously write your list? Put that person, those people, where they belong... in the past, holding their own opinion. It's *their* opinion. It's not yours to keep. Give it back to them. Move forward. You are you. Uniquely you. You have worth and value.

> And if you are not someone's cup of tea...
> Then don't drink tea together.

It's Your Own Business, Not Theirs

Becoming single again, or merely being single for any amount of time, can feel like one of the most challenging phases of life. Making decisions can feel much heavier when you are making them alone, and it's normal to question if you are doing the right thing. You will worry over everyday issues like juggling expenses and managing home repairs, to the bigger decisions of vehicle purchases and handling problems with your children. On the personal side, you'll wonder when it's appropriate to move forward with your life after death or divorce. Facing any of these areas on your own can feel daunting. You will second guess yourself more than once.

Friend, you will make mistakes. You will likely make a poor decision or two. Your lifestyle may change a little – or a lot! Your appearance might change. *You* will change. Life is different when you are single. You may want to listen to a friend or a family member's input as you find your way; however, at the end of the day, it is your life. And only you can live it.

Throughout this journey of change and finding your new normal, it may be awkward for those who have known you a long time. They won't truly understand the day-to-day struggle you are facing and will naturally form opinions about your decisions. This life is foreign to them and they simple don't live the unfolding events from your perspective. Because of this, it can cause those friends and loved ones to ask embarrassing questions, form judgments, or fire off stinging comments without warning.

I had one friend experience this even as she was in process of her divorce decision. She attended a church with tight rules and loose lips and received opinions to make your jaw drop. They began as she was experiencing marriage problems with a man who was verbally abusive and unfaithful. She was living in extreme circumstances in which no one should feel pressured to remain. The women in her circles though? They had a different opinion, telling her, "You just need to pretty yourself up!" *That* was their opinion on what steps my friend should take to make her cheating husband return home. As if she had not already experienced enough criticism and verbal abuse. My mind is blown how *anyone* can think offering an opinion like this is appropriate, much less to a woman struggling in an abusive relationship. Needless to say, my friend is now happily relocated to a wonderfully accepting and loving church. *Good for her!*

Years ago on one of the calls home to my parents, I was chatting the usual recap of my week's mini-disasters. I have the ability to be expressive, so I'm sure my story was animated to keep it interesting. My dad, thus, interpreted my animation and formed an opinion of my situation. Meaning, he formed an opinion of me being a single female living two states away from family. He then sternly responded, "You just need to come home!" Mind you, I was a grown woman, had two teens in high school, was established in a successful job, *and* owned a house in a wonderful city. I'm sure my dad was merely being protective of his only daughter; however, it struck a nerve with me. I was strong, independent, and courageous. My parents were not of the generation where they understood that some of us females actually *enjoy* making a life of our own. I had to accept that my dad held a completely different opinion of my single life.

I stood my ground and argued my case. Of course it didn't change anything and my dad held to his opinion. I also held to mine. This is how it often goes. You can argue, yes, and in the end it is simply difficult for others to comprehend the single-again life and challenges you live. This is when you evaluate the conversation and respond based on the relationship, not on the opinions or lack of understanding. If the relationship is important, you may kindly *agree to disagree*. You can love the person *and* disagree with their opinion. And then you move forward. You can also politely request that your future conversations together avoid the topic! Because in the end, their opinion is their opinion, and *your life is your business*.

Dealing with Loss

Through the years, I have observed many opinions toward those who have lost spouses. If you are a recent widow and feel ready to move on with a new relationship, you should feel free to move on. And if you need more time, take the time you need. This is a deeply personal decision which should not be manipulated by others' opinions, one way or another. It is *your* heart and we do not know what you've been through.

If you are ready to move on and you have children, including adult children, having a conversation first will allow them time to process. At any age, seeing your parent with someone else can be unsettling. This is not to say you should postpone your decision, rather, the open communication will allow them opportunity to express their feelings and adapt to the idea. Hearing their opinion will help you navigate *how* you might proceed forward.

I want to offer an additional word of encouragement for those who have lost partners to death, especially if your spouse was ill for an extended period. Others will likely not realize the strain you have endured or how long you have been without a normal active relationship. This has no reflection on the love you had for your spouse, it merely means your life has been different and you have lived through challenges beyond what most can comprehend.

> People offer their opinions to you while standing in their own shoes, not yours.

If you would like to experience partnership again, you should feel free to move forward. I had one friend say to me, "I've not been a wife for the last number of years. I've been a nurse." She adored her husband. She also had the right to be happy, to be loved again, and to enjoy life with a partner. People may raise eyebrows and offer opinions when you make the decision to move on. Yet remember, this is your personal decision and you deserve happiness again.

The "Question" Opinion

At one point, after I'd had a number of failed relationships, I started dating a new man who appeared to have great potential. As I continued dating him, someone close to me teasingly said, "Don't mess this one up!!" Ouch. As if the past breakups were all my fault?? To clarify, you date someone to learn if you are compatible. Sometimes you simply discover you are not! And thus, your single life gets extended.

The longer I went without being married, however, I began to hear a new type of opinion. This one was always voiced in the form of a question. *Why are you still single?!* Ahh, tricky. Delivering your opinion in the structure of a question! Maybe I won't notice that you are curious, or that you are wondering what is wrong with me. The question alone tells me you think someone single again should be married by this point, and I'm not.

Does anyone stop to think how we single women are supposed to answer that kind of question? *Why am I still single?* Let's see, what could be my possible answer? The first response which comes to mind, "Umm, because nobody wants me??" Or another response, "Well, how am I still single? Let me count the ways!" I suppose both of those responses would have been a bit sassy. (And no, I did not respond with either.) I quickly learned to say, "I guess I'm just picky!" Yes, part of that answer is true, but the real story was I had opportunities which did not get to that point because the men did not see a future with me. While in hindsight I'm incredibly glad those relationships did not work out, that question at the time always made me flinch.

I had to realize though, whether I had multiple short-term dating spells or whether I was still single after years alone, that did not equate to failure on my part. And neither do your similar experiences reflect failure on your part. Trust you are valuable and, when the right person comes along, you will see your worth, feel loved, and have a successful relationship once again. Breakups are not your failures alone, and others' slanted questions do not define your ability to love and be loved. You eventually learn which battles to pick; I personally chose not to take those questions to the battlefield.

Are there times when we should stand our ground, though, and provide feedback to some of the opinions and comments which are too personal or hurtful toward us? Yes, of course! Just be mindful, you may not always get the response you anticipate. I discovered, in spite of my best efforts to explain my perspective, others basically could not comprehend the complex world of single life. It wasn't really a fault of theirs, it was merely not their experience. I learned to accept I was going to have mishaps. Others may not understand and may ask awkward (sometimes inappropriate) questions. And I still had value. All of those truths can exist together.

Got Mistakes?!

I was raised in a fairly conservative environment. Growing up I can only remember one divorced person in our entire church congregation. As a young person, it always felt like divorce was *the unpardonable sin*. Even though I had later grown and moved away, I was still associated with that group of people. You can imagine, then, how much of an outcast I felt when I became divorced in my mid-thirties. When I looked around, there was no one like me. I saw no one who could relate. So I started my new different life alone.

I experienced struggles that were hidden from those around me. At that time, my greatest concern was making sure I had enough income to keep the roof over my children's heads and food in the cupboards. I had to work. A lot. And I'm certain my amazing teenagers finished raising themselves on their own because those years are a blur to me. People generally don't see our attempt at juggling work and kids, the stressful monthly bank account balance, the fears we are facing, the quiet nights we are home alone, or the thoughts we process trying to figure out how to move forward. People don't see our insecurities. Our boredom. They don't see what we see when we look in the mirror. They can't trace our endless circle of thoughts, wondering when someone will come along so we can feel connected again. They don't live the emotions or chain of events that leads us to where they view us on Sunday mornings or at the office.

> **Wherever you are, in whatever situation or pickle you find yourself, whatever your mistakes or regrets, even the self-imposed ones, remember, these are going to happen.**

Obviously, it would be best if we kept ourselves in check and could look back to see we never caved, we never blew it, we never had a moment, or a questionable season. Realistically though, we will have a moment and sometimes we do blow it. If you are a Christian, crack open your old testament. Read the life of David. Talk about making mistakes! Yet he went on to write the Psalms. Abraham took things into his own hands and really messed up. Yet God blessed the world through him. Rest assured, there is forgiveness. And there is definitely life after mistakes.

You are treading in different and difficult waters. Sometimes you will end up in the deep end. Other times, the waves might crash up over you unexpectedly. When that happens, there is no need to feel ashamed or embarrassed, just tread to safer waters! Whether it is a bad relationship, a mistake with your children, or bad financial choices. When you catch that you're in a problem, try to find someone to help and then work on a solution. If people don't understand how you got there, well, they can be grateful their life treads in a better current.

Remember that conservative upbringing I mentioned? Even though I was older and my kids were married, I actually lived with someone for a few years. My mom had a hard time grasping my decision and didn't even want her best friend to know. While I can respect that my choices may not have been God's best for me, I have come to accept it is okay to be imperfect.

There was also more to my story my mom couldn't have fully understood because she wasn't walking in my shoes. First of all, at that time, I had been eating dinner alone for 15 years. Fifteen years. That's approximately 5,475 dinners either alone or with someone non-committed to me. And that's just dinner. That is 16,425 meals without a partner. Quite frankly, it was nice to have someone who purely enjoyed dinner at home and watching TV with me.

There were other events contributing to my decision, as well. I had an upstairs pipe break which caused the first floor of my house to be gutted to the frame. I had no home for 6 months that year. I also had a surgery where I needed weeks of help during my recovery. These are the kind of life events people often don't realize a single person may be facing alone. While my choices back then were not my mother's idea of best choices, I had contributing factors that I'm certain almost no one realized I was facing. Regardless of the opinions and judgments, the bottom line is, I was an adult and free to make decisions without anyone attempting to place guilt on my already very lonely, challenging, frustrating life.

While I truly want to encourage you to seek God's best in your life, please know you will face overwhelming challenges alone and you quite honestly may make mistakes! When this happens, there will be people who do not understand. There will be opinions spoken. There might be heaps of guilt. Do you think I am even able to write these words without feeling some of that guilt still? I can almost picture my old friends reading these words and their minds conjuring up so many other ways I could have gotten myself through those challenges. The reality, though? No one has walked in my shoes. And no one has walked in yours.

Perhaps this is why Jesus told us to *not judge* and then went on to remind us that we, too, would be judged... *by our own measuring stick!*

Although I forget the topic and even the person, I remember a response once when a friend replied to me with, "No judgment here!" I will always remember how welcome and forgiving that statement made me feel. I have tried to pay it forward using that phrase many times over through the years. What a kind soul who allowed me to be human that day. That phrase offers neither approval nor disapproval. It is purely opinion free and judgment free.

It would be nice if our friends and loved ones would also embrace that phrase, minimizing their opinions and advice toward us. Realistically, though, people don't always embrace the judgment-free zone. You will likely catch a few zingers thrown at you or witness a disapproving face. I hope you have the personality type where you can brush off the criticisms and let them go. Unfortunately, I think for most of us, opinions sting. I know it and I've lived it. I urge you, please, work through comments which are hurtful or cause self-doubt and then try to let it go. My dear friend, those people don't deserve your attention, and you are worth so much more than their opinion of you.

NEXT STEPS

Something to think about...

Biting opinions can spring up from those around you who have not walked in your shoes. When they do, make this your mantra:

"Their opinion does not define me. *God* defines me."

Something to move forward...

Think about opinions you've had a hard time shaking off. What could be the reasons for that person to have voiced them? Additionally, what opinions have inaccurately molded you??

Something to do...

Ferociously write any hurtful or absurd opinions you've received from others. If they are valid, what could you potentially change? If they are not valid, is it perhaps time to burn the paper along with the control these opinions have had over you?

If you don't have a fireplace, I recommend stepping outside for this cleansing ceremony.

5

Friendship and Friend "Shifts"

When we are married or partnered, our friendships, along with our lifestyles, generally match those of our social network. Our coupled pieces fit neatly together. It's natural. Typical weekends might look like this: The guys in the family room watching a game. The girls in the kitchen are putting food together and chatting about kids, work, or new recipes. Dinner nights out? Table for four. Meeting up at parties? Together. Two pair of tickets for events. Wedding reception tables? Always set for six or eight! *Even* numbers.

Then, life happens, and you find yourself single again. Your comfortable even number becomes odd. Odd, numerically, and well, odd as in awkward. Lopsided. Dinners out leave an empty chair around the table or an empty bench seat. Trying to play games and going to events leaves one person alone. Outings cause one of the persons to divide their conversation uncomfortably between the two others. Or other couples start to get invited to come along, and the single person becomes the fifth wheel. Eventually, lifestyles change, invites dwindle, coupled friends spend more time with other coupled friends. *Friendshift* happens.

Friendshifts. Have you heard this phrase or the concept of it? I thought my creative mind made up that catchy word. It turns out it is already a word. Different from my definition though, friendshifting is defined as intentional, something chosen. A process whereby you evaluate a friendship and make a calculated decision to *shift* away from it.

Realistically, however, when we become single again, friendshift can happen (and frequently does) whether we want it to or not. There is no planning. There is no evaluation. There is no choice. It does not happen overnight. It does not necessarily come in one defining incident or with any intention. Additionally, there will likely be a few painful moments in the process. I can't genuinely say there is any pleasant way to experience loss and change in friendships. It is truly sad, and it is natural to miss how things used to be.

So what now? When you begin losing a friend, how do you turn the ship when it feels like that friend ship is veering off course? Or maybe you sense the ship is simply sinking altogether. Realistically, this change in course is natural. Life may be telling you it's time to walk through the open door and move forward. Or rather, hop on board and venture new seas.

> **For many of us, the transition of friendship is easier said than done.**

When friendships begin to fade, it's not pleasant to move on. There will be days when sulking with that bowl of ice cream and a good movie is the desirable option rather than pulling yourself up and seeking new friendships. I understand, it's the easier option yes, but healthy? Only infrequently. You may not feel like you want new friends. Your social circle might be small. Your church possibly offers limited options with anyone who suits your style. Losing a friend you loved, trusted, and enjoyed is hard to replace and you may feel like you are simply not up to the task.

Well, I agree, thinking of replacing a good friend with someone new is a rather disheartening thought. Frankly, some friendships feel simply irreplaceable. If you feel this way, maybe you could view a new friend as an *addition* rather than a replacement.

Meeting a new friend will be different, yes, and maybe that's a good thing! A new friend can add a fresh layer of perspective to your life. Someone different will bring interests that might nudge you to try new activities. Gaining a friend has a long list of benefits. So put that pack of ice cream back in the freezer. Or better yet, *consider inviting someone new over to share a scoop!* The biggest favor you might end up doing for yourself is to accept the changes life is bringing and embrace new possibilities. It may be challenging at first; however, the sooner you acknowledge this natural progression of friendshift, the healthier you will feel about moving forward.

Building New Friendships

I always enjoy my trips back home, and I make an intentional effort to reconnect with close family friends from my past on my visits. We have a familiarity that makes conversation easy. We have memories that always bring laughter. And we have the same values which allows an understanding with each other. Those friendships run deep and are cherished beyond measure. Those kind of friendships also grow and develop over time.

If I'm not careful, I can find myself shying away from investing in new friendships because they aren't quite as similar or compatible to those of my past. If you face this same hurdle, I encourage you to run toward it, spring up, and take that leap! The past, with its memories and comforts is always going to be there. As harsh as this might sound, I want to remind you, you are living in the *present.* And in this present, some of your friendships will be new ones. Will it maybe take some time to settle in to finding things in common? Will you possibly bump into pain points unknowingly? Are you going to have slightly differing values or beliefs? Yes, I'm almost certain of it. As you get to know them, though, you will discover common interests. You will come to value having someone to spend time, check in, and share experiences.

If this is all sounding a bit outside your comfort zone, I completely understand! Oddly, I have a rather shy streak so this is a personal area I have had to work on myself. However, I can attest, taking that first step can be more rewarding than you could ever imagine.

A number of years back, I had moved to a new suburb. As I was also recently single again *again*, I was experiencing friendshift in my social life. If you ever meet me in person, you will think I do not have a shy bone in my body and you might guess I would easily conquer my own *friendshift* experience. Reality though? When it comes to getting myself out there and making new friends, virtually every bone in my body is a shy one.

I can speak in front of a thousand people with no fear. Business dinner with a CEO? Piece of cake! But seeking out a new friend in my personal life? Just curl me up in a blanket with my Breyers and Netflix! I tell you this so you know if I can step outside of my comfort zone and make friends, you can, too!

Here's how I once did this when I was in a new community and working long hours in my day life: In our small suburb we had a Facebook page. One Saturday (after an hour of getting up my nerve), I posted a simple question asking if anyone knew if there were single groups in our area for mid-age adults. I was expecting to get a few suggestions I might try. Much to my surprise, not only were there no single groups for older adults, but all kinds of people began chiming in saying they would love it if we had a group. *Then* the replies changed into asking me to START a singles group for our area! Oh my!! Did I mention the thing about my comfort zone???

That experience revealed more surprises than I could have imagined. First, I had *no idea* there were so many older singles in my direct area. I had no idea how many people were bored and hungry for friendship in their lives. Why were they bored and hungry? Because they had friendshift happen to them also! Next, I would not have guessed how many people were willing to step up and help me create our Facebook group. And lastly, I never anticipated the fun and friendships I would gain from taking that simple step outside my comfort zone. That simple question on Facebook led me to a group of new friends where the effects of our friendshifting disappeared. We had community again and we had it with people walking in our shoes. An added bonus, even though I have since moved away... I still have some of those friendships to this day!

Whatever fear or procrastination you are facing about finding new friends, please, I urge you, please step out and start a conversation! Ask someone if they would like to grab coffee sometime. Maybe you can start a book club. I've not yet learned to play pickleball, but I know others who have made friends through that favorite activity. Maybe your church would support starting a new bible study group for middle-aged singles. Is there a neighbor you see walking who you might engage in conversation? Is there a smile or a helping hand you could offer someone? There are others out there walking in your same shoes who would love to have a new friend. Look around and see who might be waiting for an invitation.

If the thought of all this freezes you in your tracks, you are not alone! In the next chapter I'll go into more detail about how I worked through my own fears. Even though stepping out to make new friends can be hard, the reality is friendships *do* shift and new friendships *are* valuable. Remember, there are others walking in your shoes who would love to have a new friend, too.

Friendshifting as a Single

In my first paragraphs regarding this concept of *friendshift*, I explained how it evolves rather naturally in our lives when we go from the coupled life to the uncoupled single life. This cycle, however, can repeat itself in other ways, as well. Sometimes the shifting will happen within your circle of single friends.

> **We've all heard the saying that people come into our life for a reason, a season, or a lifetime. If there was ever a moment to embrace that thought, this is the time.**

As you begin to enjoy the company of other single friends, it will be wise to understand that one of them may begin dating. In the beginning, it will have little impact on your friendship. As their new relationship progresses, though, you will begin to experience a difference in your conversations. Initially, your friend may be excited or nervous about meeting someone and, naturally, they will want to share the details with you. This can be fun and you might even feel like you're back in high school again (in a good way). Then, if the relationship moves deeper, your friend will have a difficult time dividing their schedule with you and their new date.

Please realize, *this is not personal!* There are, after all, still 24 hours in the day. Try to support your friend and understand this is simply a natural part of life.

When a friend starts dating, you may feel other emotions creep in, as well. As your friend shares their new experience or you see their social media posts smiling with the new partner, slight pangs of envy might sock you with a few jabs. You want to be happy for them and yet here you are still alone. Sans partner. Single. Solo. Their stories and posts can feel like salt poured into a wound. Then, what follows is what you have gone through before... times together dwindle, conversations become less frequent, and the shape of your lives begin to match less and less. You experience it fresh, again. Friendshift.

If you are still peeking through these pages trying to find where I hid those magic potions for a problem-free single life, you may want to read my introduction again. My intent is to help you *navigate* these waters of single life, not hoist your whole ship out of the ocean!

Am I trying to say your new friendships have no guarantee of shifting on you? That sounds a bit blunt, yet I have to be honest. Yes, I am saying they could shift. People do meet partners when they least expect it. When that happens, schedules and lifestyles simply change. Is that to say making new friends is a futile effort? Absolutely not! And while there are no fairy dust packets here to sprinkle away this phenomenon, we *can* work on ways to make friendshifting and flying solo a little more manageable.

Navigating Friendshift

Knowing that life is somewhat unpredictable and friendships may reshape themselves, it's important to get one step ahead to minimize the discomfort when this happens. The solution is, more than anything, common sense. (No magic ingredients required.)

To help soften possible friendshifts, consider building a small *group* of single friends around you. Depending on your age, interests, and personality, I know this could be a stretch for you. This is when it might be good to join some type of organized group. You might consider a singles group, book club, sports activity, community networking, etc. Joining a group allows you to step in and easily surround yourself with a number of people. As you do this, when one of them begins dating, their shift will be much less noticeable as you will still be surrounded with other friendships.

When *Your* Ship Shifts!

To this point, I've talked mostly about the experience where your friends begin shifting away from you. The reality is, there are going to be times in your life when *you* may be the one shifting away from others! I want to reiterate here, friendshift does not necessarily fall into one category of negative versus positive. It simply sometimes happens. It is natural, if it is not merely functional. We cannot possibly hold onto every friend we have ever met along the way. Perhaps stay in touch through social media, yes. But to keep up with activities and personal regular conversations? There are not enough hours in the day for that. And when your time comes... when you meet someone... when that special person wants to spend more time with you... *you* will friendshift away from others.

Be prepared, there may be some guilt when this happens. You are going to have a friend want to do something with you, and your new date will be wanting you. You'll have to decide. How do you split your time? They may even attempt to place some guilt on you, intentional or not. This is all natural. As you work through this transition, I encourage you to be gentle on your friends.

If you feel comfortable, you may want to have a conversation with your friend. Let them know you value the friendship and you would also like to explore this new relationship. (Take note: I'm intentionally recommending the word *and* rather than *but* for your conversation.) You can both value a friendship *and* have a desire to explore a new relationship at the same time!

Let them know you are doing your best to navigate the changes while balancing your schedule. Rather than losing your friend completely, maybe you consider shifting your time with them. If you have weekly chats, consider moving to a monthly catch-up. If your Saturday nights are now tied up, what about planning a brunch or shopping day with your friend? Then, when you are with them, try to keep the focus on *them*. You will be excited about your new relationship and, remember, that could be salt in their wound. Seeing you with a new partner could bring a mix of emotions for them. They will be happy for you yet discouraged that it is not happening for them. Being considerate will go a long way to help preserve the relationship with your friend. And you will want to remain mindful, if this new dating relationship does not work out, you will want to know you still have the support of your friend!

If there was a magic formula to maintaining friendships, I would say the core ingredients should include consideration, intention, and creativity. My paths in life have certainly taken different directions throughout the years and I know how difficult it is to keep up. I leverage social media, texting, and planning calls when I know I'll have open time in my schedule. You will be surprised how much those small efforts allow you to keep your relationships when paths of life separate you. Even though I have moved out of state away from many of my close friends, several of them have arranged a visit when they've been in my area. I wouldn't trade one of those reunions for the world.

Friendshifting is sometimes caused by a limit of time or space, but our friend*ships* can be there forever.

NEXT STEPS

Something to think about...

Describe the feelings you experienced when you've had friends shift away from you. *Now, tuck those feelings away. One day they will help you be more sensitive when it's your time to shift.*

Something to move forward...

Dynamics change and so do some of our friendships. Can you accept this is part of life? The sooner you resolve to look *forward*, the sooner you will be open to new relationships.

Something to do...

The next time you are outside walking or at church... or the dog park... wherever you go alone... specifically look around to see who you might offer a hello or a smile to. Chapter 6 offers more pointers. For now, looking around is a good start!

Practice (out loud) how you might kick off a conversation with someone new.

6

Stepping Out

Everything in life seems to have instructions these days! Have you noticed that? You open a package, pull out that white pamphlet, check to make sure all the items are included, grab any tools listed, and then you start with STEP ONE. Whether I am building a bookshelf or assembling a new blender, I know the box is going to have that white instruction manual with step-by-step directions. It might take 30 minutes or it might take 3 hours yet, by the time I get to the last step, I am successfully ready to use my new product! There are instructions on how to wash each article of clothing in my closet. A step-by-step guide pops up every time I need to replace the printer cartridges. Even my new toothbrush came with an instruction video!

We have instructions for seemingly every product or task on the planet. Yet, when we were thrown into this serious transition of living single, this life-altering event that tossed us into completely new patterns, there was no white manual handed to us with that large print STEP ONE to get us started.

Oh, if it could be that simple. Realistically, though, it is not. I remember my first months of being single again. Decades now and yet some of those experiences are still crystal clear in my mind. I had married young and was married for almost 17 years when I divorced.

All I knew was married life. Even though we obviously had hit some rough patches, I had never truly thought about what my days would be like alone. I had not considered how I would go about adapting to a quiet house, adjusting to a new schedule, or parenting lopsided with only one of us at home. Where was my step-by-step for this?

To complicate things, we had been quite involved in our church which, of course, was family focused. I remember that first Sunday attending the service alone. I remember sitting in the row by myself, surrounded in a sea of couples, with no partner beside me. I felt so out of place. Although I didn't realize it at the time, my mind played tricks and exaggerated my thoughts into epic proportion. I knew I was sticking out like a sore thumb. I knew everyone was staring at me. I knew it was obvious there was empty space around me.

I can still see the families walking out afterwards. As if it were just this past Sunday, I can see the gravel and grass of that parking lot, parents with children, shuffling the family into their cars. My kids were away visiting family and I had no one. Absolutely no one. No one to talk to. No one to walk out with. No one hopping into my car. I remember how sad and alone I felt thinking about how all of the families would go home and have Sunday dinner together. They would have each other to laugh with and spend the afternoon. I would get in my car alone. I would drive home alone. I would eat Sunday dinner. Alone.

Surrounded by wonderfully kind people, I was generally outgoing and bubbly. But those first weeks? I was withdrawn, embarrassed, and empty. I didn't know how to go to church alone! If someone has not experienced this, it might sound like the most ridiculous thing. It is not ridiculous, though. Was I supposed to act as if nothing changed? Were others skeptical to talk with me? Did the situation make them uncomfortable? These were the questions storming in my head. Where was my *Going to Church Alone* instruction guide?

Whether it's returning to church or going to an office party, those first experiences walking into social settings alone can feel beyond awkward. Cringe-worthy if I'm being completely transparent here. When you have been in a marriage or long-term relationship, there are common life events you do together without even thinking. Church and parties might seem like some of the big ones. There are others, though, that can sneak up on you without warning. As trivial as they may seem, they can be just as big. Going out to eat. Seeing a movie. A routine trip to the mall. What about community festivals? Going to music events or shows? Neighborhood gatherings?

Stepping out solo those first times can be extremely challenging.

In all my years, I still do not feel comfortable showing up to social events alone, regardless of how small they are. These activities are certainly the everyday ordinary times of life; yet it can be a mountain of a struggle doing it alone.

Well-meaning people might give advice to simply do things with a friend or take one of your kids. While that sounds like a logical solution, that often turns out to be easier said than done. To begin, I don't know about you but my kids, at any age, do not want to go to many of my social functions. So please, if that's been one of your go-to considerations, do them a favor, and let's work through another solution! Even if your kids might enjoy some of your events, be mindful of the potential expectation or burden it could inadvertently place on them. It's not the best idea and, frankly, not fair.

Then there is the best friend option. Do you have a friend who is always available? I have a feeling even your best friend will likely have limits and conflicts. At some point between natural *friendshifting* and building new relationships, realistically you will face seasons where you are simply alone. There are going to be times when there is no option but to live your life and show up solo.

How then, do you pull yourself together to do this?

STEP ONE: Simply "Step Out"

I'm aware there cannot truly be a full *Single-again Instruction Manual.* (Although that would be terrific!) No, our stories and personal readiness are individually unique to our situations. That said, there is a Step One which does fit all of us venturing into social life. It is simply: *Take the first step to launch yourself!*

If this sounds extremely basic (and somewhat fearful), it is. This simple step is not always an easy one. Stepping out into life solo can be the hardest experience. If you have no idea where to even begin, that's okay! Though we don't have a full manual to reference, we can definitely talk through ideas on how to get yourself out socially and more comfortably! How to put one foot in front of the other when you really don't feel like it. How to launch yourself into some type of bearable, normal activity of living life as a single.

While everyone's single life is uniquely different, there is one common element which holds true in every single's story. It is the reality of being alone and, like it or not, facing the everyday parts of life without a partner. Later in this book we explore the different experiences you might face as you journey through single life. While those experiences will come at different times for everyone, at this moment, the everyday life waits for no one!

Though you may have days when you really do not want to get out of bed, I know you will do it anyway. You will go to work or church or the grocery store or connect with your social network. You will be around people and you will get invited to functions.

Ahh, the dreaded social functions. THIS is where your legs might freeze. Your mind may fire off an emphatic *No!* – You'll go to the store because you have to, but to a party? No. No desire for parties or meet 'n greets or any social gathering for that matter. Your pulse may be increasing right now just thinking about it! I get it!! I do get it. It's a dilemma for sure.

I might actually desire a polar plunge more than going to a group event by myself.

I also know it is healthy to get out. There are friendships waiting out there which will become invaluable along this journey. I know I want you to live life. I want you to walk in a room with your chin up, confident, and looking forward to being there. You may, though, not have the slightest desire to accept an invitation right now. Or, like me in those early days, you may not know how to get out there and take those first steps of doing life solo.

Let's explore, then, some scenarios and ideas to help minimize this anxiety. *Minimize*, meaning to reduce, to decrease. If you are thinking, "Ah-ha! This is the section that's going to offer the magic formula for taking away all my solo-in-the-room jitters!" Ouch, no. Remember, I mentioned earlier I didn't have any fairy dust packets tucked in these pages. We will, though, look at some ideas to help you see that it is truly OKAY to show up at events alone. You can learn to *step out* and make your entrance to the world in confidence!

IDEA #1

Before you even reach the point of heading out the door for a social activity, you may feel defeated about attending the function in the first place. Your mind can fill with all sorts of doubt and insecurity. Let's begin, then, by tackling those unwieldy voices running through your head. Those thoughts will try to talk you out of the event by telling you how awkward it is going to be. You might have numerous sound tracks firing off. For now, though, let's concentrate on one of the main tracks. Yep, it's the one telling you everyone will stare at you and you're going to stick out like a sore thumb.

Join me, then, in a little exercise:

Think of the last time you were at a social event and saw someone alone. (Pause. Got that visual?) Now think of the last time you stared at someone alone while thinking, "Oh that poor soul just got divorced!" Note: If you have done that, shame on you! Bad form. (Although, I seriously doubt you have ever done that.) Next, thinking of someone who has recently lost their partner by death, did you merely gawk at them across the room? Please answer no to that question. My guess is, you're a decent human being and you probably spent time talking with them to help them adjust. So remember this and realize, people are not staring. If they are, you might consider finding a new group of friends to associate with!

Even if your partner left you and you are feeling inadequate, you can feel confident and remind yourself that you are a worthy person. Just because you don't have a date or a plus-one, it simply means that right now you are living solo. I would much rather be known for being selective and alone, rather than having an unsuitable person attached for partnership sake. Remove the voices. Walk tall and feel confident that you are a complete person.

IDEA #2

Even after a good "pep talk to self," there still comes that moment of physically walking out the door and heading alone to a social function. *Enter brain's cringe emotion, taking its place front and center stage.* Yes, seriously, at this point the brain's cringe emotion does enter center stage!

I was going to be comical and use the phrase "enter stage right," and then I wondered, "Hmm. Where does cringing enter the brain exactly?" I am writing this entire book from my own experiences and personal conversations – because I've had plenty of both. However, I found an actual article on cringing and it is associated with social settings! Wow, who knew. [–*The Neuroscience of Cringe: Why the Past Still Burns*, by Walter Donway] To help minimize that awkwardly physical emotion, then, here is an idea that is both easy and casual. I don't know about you, but easy and casual is always a good approach for me.

If you know some people who will be attending the event or church service, reach out to them in advance. Simply ask them, "Hey, could I beg a small favor? I'm still adjusting to showing up at things alone. Could I sit with you or pop over if I run out of people to mingle with?" – That request is not too intrusive and it will help you relax going into the event knowing you have a safety net.

I once did this for our big company Christmas event. It was four months after my divorce, so I was really in those beginning stages. Even though I would know basically everyone attending the party and it was being held at the very gorgeous Union Station in downtown Nashville, my skin was crawling with the decision to attend. I did not want to go! I did not want to step through those doors by myself into a sea of people dressed to the nines and mingling freely with each other. Then again, did I want to go home after work to my quiet house and sit sadly all night long knowing I was missing out on all the fun, food, and music? I ended up telling someone from our site that I was skeptical about going alone. They reassured me they would be there and it would be okay. And though I was still a tad nervous, I went home, dressed, and made myself walk through those foreboding doors. Before I even had the need to find my friend, someone else spotted me first and walked up with a big hug and welcomed me! It was much easier than I thought, and I even had a funny thing happen. Somehow, I guess in trying to chit-chat, I got asked for a date by a man who wasn't even part of our event! And no, I did not take him up on the offer. Nonetheless, it made for a great laugh. Obviously, the night went much better than expected, and all it took was that one small conversation to let someone know I had butterflies.

IDEA #3

When attending a social function, it is always easy to head to the food or drink line. This is a super simple trick to help you get settled into the occasion. People are often in those areas solo anyway, and it's easy to pick a small conversation to get started. Comment on the food, the music, décor, or the hosts. Compliment someone's outfit. Ask about their connection to the event. These are simple starter topics that can help get your vocal cords out of a jam.

As I was writing this chapter, I happened to have a doctor's appointment already scheduled that week. Sitting in the waiting room, I had someone compliment my purse. We ended up having a nice conversation and then she agreed to meet for coffee to contribute to my book research. It turns out I met a lovely person who merely liked my purse!

In a worst case scenario, let's say you find yourself at a function with absolutely no one you know and no one seemingly interested in trivial chit-chat. Keep your cell phone handy! This is the time to pull it out and text someone.

> **No worries if you have no one to text. I don't generally encourage dishonesty, but if you must pretend... Well, I can't say I've never done that before.**

Then, if we're really being sneaky, you could set an alarm on your phone to go off at a certain time that sounds like your ringtone. Okay, maybe that one is taking it a bit far, but hey, we are generating ideas here. Brainstorming is good!

Also remember, you do not have to be the first to arrive and you certainly don't have to stay for an entire event. It is okay to have a few trial runs until you become more comfortable doing life single! For church, sit somewhere different or maybe near the back in case you really feel like slipping out. Trust me, there are worse things in life. I promise no one will know the reason you've had to leave.

IDEA #4

Practice going solo! Intentionally pre-plan and try out some uncomfortable situations alone. Is there a restaurant you would like to try and haven't had the chance? I often take a book or small notepad so I'm not sitting in my seat staring into space while I'm waiting for the food. I used to avoid going out to eat by myself. Then it dawned on me, these people don't know if I'm single or traveling for work!

If I were on a business trip, I would be eating alone not giving it a second thought. And I would take a book to keep from being bored.

I remember years ago, being at the beach alone writing in a notebook. I literally had someone come up who had been watching me and asked if I was writing a book! Now, that made me feel special. Nonetheless, I was on a solo trip by choice. It was a wonderful mini-vacation taking time away from my busy career to simply breathe for a few days. Because I *chose* to make that trip alone, I didn't feel lonely, unworthy, or intimidated at all. That was such a confirmation of how our *mindset* can literally make or break the experience we have. Although I know I will never be at a 100% comfort level going out alone, I can definitely see I've come a long way from those first solo ventures.

Stepping Back In

Whether you get invited out or decide to try your own personal trial runs, be prepared, there will be places that stir up past emotions and make the event difficult. It could be something as simple as going back to your favorite Chinese restaurant or as big as going on that cruise you never got around to taking with your partner. Unfortunately, life is not so simple that either one of these situations may be avoided forever. Whatever your special place or event might be, when it comes time to cross that path, take time to process your emotions so that you can enjoy it with either yourself or a new friend.

My worst experience with this was on a first date after I had gone through an incredibly sad breakup. A really nice guy had asked me to go to the movies, which I dearly love to do! What I hadn't realized, though, was that I loved doing it with my former partner and really hadn't gone to movies with anyone but him. It was quite emotional taking that first step with someone new. So much so that I cried *while* I was getting ready!

What did I do, then?? Well, I took some deep breaths, wiped my face dry, put on a smile, stepped out my front door, and went to the movies! It's odd but, thinking back, I don't recall a day of movie sadness past that one time. Maybe it just took facing the situation to see I could do it and still be happy.

To this day I still love the big screens and giant popcorn buckets... and I have even been to a movie or two by myself. It's not all that fun, *and nor is it the end of the world.*

Whether it is that favorite routine you had with your partner or a destination you can't possibly picture alone, be careful to ensure you still allow yourself the fun and relaxation you deserve. If it seems too unbearable, maybe you consider a variation. That might mean a new restaurant on a different side of town. If it is something as major as a destination, you could change hotels, explore a different beach, or check out that museum you always wanted to try. If you want support, take a trusted friend. It's okay to step slowly when you're unsure, but whatever you do, please step back in!

> Regardless of the reason that you are now single again, you deserve to be happy and enjoy all this world has to offer. Sure it will be different, and it will take some adjusting. I can't sugarcoat that. Nor can I provide a manual with magical step-by-step instructions. Hang in there, though, and keep putting yourself out there. You *will* find your way.

NEXT STEPS

Something to think about...

For what situation in your single journey do you wish there were a Step-by-Step Manual to guide you?

Something to move forward...

What potential areas or events from your past might trigger sadness? What could you do differently to help adjust into your new normal?

Something to do...

Think of one hurdle you would like to successfully get over. In your journal, brainstorm specific ways you can accomplish this. Write in detail the how, where, when, and who will be there to help.

I know how much moving forward might hurt,
I know living solo can feel daunting at times.
I've prayed for you as you take these steps.

7

Household of ONE

"Could you pick up a gallon of milk on your way home tonight?"

"The yard looks great. Thanks for mowing before the rain hit!"

"Honey, could you reach my special dish on that top shelf?"

"I just had someone rear-end me. Can you come pick me up?"

"Will you run to the gas station before we head out tomorrow?"

"Ohh! There's water all over the floor! Quick, grab some towels!"

"I'll change the sheets if you can vac before Mom arrives."

When we are living single again, these "partner" phrases are no longer active in our vocabulary. The single person has to dial a friend, rely on the kids, pester a neighbor, pay for help, or simply figure it out on their own.

Do people realize??? In our single world, there is no one around to ask a favor or trade a chore. Emergencies are no longer handled with a quick extra pair of hands. And if you're anything like me, it's hard to ask for help. I don't like to bother people. They have their own family, their own dilemmas, their own busy schedules. So in my decades alone, I worked at basically figuring out how to handle almost everything on my own. Other people commented on how strong I was. I even had the nickname of Wonder Woman!

Then again, hmm, what else was I to do?! That yard wasn't going to mow itself. That dead light bulb wasn't going to mystically start glowing again. And nope, that old dingy wall paint was not going to magically change colors on me overnight. Granted, I might possess a few mad skills in the tool shed, but still, what were the options??

On the average single income, you can't simply go paying for something every time there's a break or you want your home freshened up. *I certainly couldn't.* So I asked a lot of questions, I learned, and I did what had to be done. Needless to say, the guys at the home improvement store got to know me fairly well.

> Was it overwhelming at times? Were there tears?
> Did I get exhausted? YES.

While I accepted my situation and was willing to learn and do, I have to say there is one one thing I wish married people realized (or remembered) about their single friends and family. I wish they realized that singles are solely responsible for everything in their world! There is no *you-wash-I'll-dry* teamwork happening in a single's home. There is no Honey Do list hanging on the refrigerator. No second vehicle to use in an emergency. Whatever needs done, whatever disaster pops up, the single person simply shoulders all of it and has to figure it out.

Even in the work environment, I've seen companies lean on single people to pick up extra hours or hint for them to work holidays. What in the world?! That makes no sense.

If you are feeling overwhelmed with responsibilities or worn out because there is so much to do, please know this is normal and it wears on you. I can remember a time when my lawn mower had given out on me, so I purchased a new one. Little did I realize how heavy it would be – or that it would require actual *assembly!*

During that time, I was working long hours so it was evening when I got started. I was thinking I would simply fill the mower with gas and get the yard finished before dark. *That* did not happen and it was well after dark by the time I gave up. I was completely exhausted from my long work day and then had become fully drained emotionally from that impossible assembly. I'm certain there were other life pressures piled on me, as well, and this recent dilemma was my last straw. Not knowing how to safely release all the built-up frustrations by that late night hour, I remember going into the garage and grabbing my big corn broom. Walking back out to the street while sobbing uncontrollably, I heaved that long broom over and over and over again on the curb of the driveway. And when I had finished, I sat down on the edge of the drive and cried some more.

While that may sound to some like a crazed human, I have a feeling you might be relating. It just *piles* up until you snap and you can take no more.

Becoming single, you learn very quickly that pretty much *everything* under the roof (and in the yard) becomes your full responsibility. If you had a lot or even a little support from your previous partner, most likely there was a second set of hands to help with assembling new items, assisting around the house, or running a quick errand. Whether it was assisting with a minor repair, folding a few towels, or emptying the trash, there was at least someone around to pitch in. Even if you lived with a lazy person, there were likely two extra hands available when you really needed them. Even if you were only dating, those hands were likely ready to jump in when you truly had to have help. Living single is not only lonely, it can also be physically taxing and emotionally exhausting.

Does My Family Understand?

If this book falls into the hands of friends or relatives who have single family members, it is my hope they will capture a glimpse of a day-in-the-life of their single loved one. I'm not sure they can grasp all that their single family member has on the plate. *It's full!*

It's the simple things that pile up when you are living in that household of one... grabbing the mail, taking out the trash, cleaning bathrooms, running the vacuum, dusting, cooking meals, dabbing up spills, rinsing dishes, washing laundry, paying bills, changing sheets, doing the yard work, shopping for groceries, filling the tank, handling car maintenance... plus how many etceteras have I left off? It's not that I wish pity from your married friends and family. Not that at all. I simply want them to have a better understanding of the daily life under your roof doing it alone.

Outside of the day-to-day responsibilities, there was another area really tough on me: Finances! Especially around the holidays. Whether there is one or two of us living in the house, there are going to be the same number of trick-or-treaters looking for goodies this year. And Christmas? Ouch, that one really hit my purse strings.

For many years, our family stuck to the tradition of getting gifts for everyone. I have two older brothers. They're great and loving, by the way. Back in those early divorced years, though, wow it was hard. They were each married with their double incomes, and they each had 3 kids. I only had 2 kids. So there I was on my single income buying for 10 extra people, while they had their double incomes buying for only 8 extras. Do you see where that math fell a little lopsided on my single income budget?? Boy was I grateful for the year we switched over to drawing names!

I guess I could have spoken up, but did I want to be the poo-poo person to change our whole family tradition because I was the only one who couldn't afford Christmas? *No.* I had never been a woe-is-me person and wasn't about to start. So I carried on to make it work. My family had no idea how much I cried each Christmas trying to come up with enough money for all the extra gifts. These are the types of situations I wish couples could understand regarding the single's life.

Or maybe our families think our expenses are lower because we're living "single." But do they realize, when that pipe breaks and I have to call a plumber, he's going to charge me $200 whether there's been one or two of us using that sink. Same repair expense but coming out of one income. Or do they think being single, I'm saving on the electric bill? Umm, maybe?? If I turn the heat down in the winter and throw on an extra sweater – or cut the AC back in July and strip down to my tank top! I've tried things like this and, quite frankly, it's uncomfortable and frustrating.

Hopefully, you have not had to experience the pressure of keeping up with your dual-income family members. My guess is, you probably have also had those same expectations. Whether it has been implied, or self-inflicted from something rooted within your being, it is time to shift your thinking and take care of yourself. If you have family expecting you to show up at that reunion with the same batch of goodies they're bringing, feel free to alter your contribution next summer. And hold zero guilt for it!

You don't need to bring attention; just bring less food! Chances are, no one will even notice or say a word. If they do, wow. We'll have to pray for them. If you feel you do want to say something beforehand, the conversation might sound like this, "Hey, just a reminder, now that I'm flying solo, I have all the same bills but half the income, so I'm going to be a little more frugal with my contributions this year." There. Done. Show up with what you can. Enjoy your family and all that good fried chicken!

Emotions and Finances

I know the topic of finances can stir up a myriad of feelings. Single life and your household-of-one budget brings a bundle of financial decisions all wrapped in a *bundle* of emotions. Embarrassment. Anger. Fear. Frustration. Isolation. Just to name a few. If you've experienced ANY of these, it is okay and it is normal. It happens to most of us at one point or another.

Managing a home, whether renting or owning, kids or no kids, pets or not, when your income is cut, it can get tough. I've learned this can happen whether you've become alone through divorce, domestic partnership, or death. The bottom line is, regardless of how you got here, you may have been left in a financial struggle. If that has happened to you, it can bring out all kinds of feelings and trigger reactions you might not have even known you had down inside.

If you have been left in a less-than-desirable situation, it may not be a story you feel comfortable sharing. You may very well be facing these frustrations completely alone. Remember, though, while you are facing them alone, you truly are *not* alone. There are many, many others walking in your shoes.

If you have not grieved your financial loss, I want to encourage you to do this. Acknowledge your anger and fears, even if you can only do this privately behind closed doors. THEN, once you've accepted your anger and frustration, please take steps to move forward. If you harbor your bitterness, the only person who will suffer is YOU. Neither the person nor the situation is worth bringing harm to yourself. Holding on will impact your emotions, your physical health, and your relationships. No person is worthy of stealing that, too! Let go of your bitterness. Holding on will not make things any easier. Take a moment to fully vent the frustration of your situation. Then, move on.

Action, not anger, is the best step! I know there are organizations like Dave Ramsey Solutions that can be a good resource to help you get back on track financially. Ramsey's *Financial Peace University* is a game changer. If needed, you can attend FPU remotely. The course is led by caring people, it's easy to understand, and it's actually even fun. An added bonus – you will find community in the class group!

> Regardless of where you are, work to take charge of your circumstances rather than allowing those circumstances to have charge over you.

Juggle, Struggle or Make a Plan

There are the financial struggles, family dynamics, and home responsibilities I've mentioned so far. And then there is the day-today detail surrounding each of these areas. If you have kids at home, add the juggle of homework, school lunches, overnights, and carpool duty, not to mention extra laundry, fussy eaters, snappy behavior, and messes in every nook ‘n cranny. There is no one to run to the store when you’re missing that ingredient in the batch of cookies you’re mixing. – You take an hour out of your schedule or simply shelve the recipe. Then, kids or not, there are the home repairs. You either quickly become very very handy or you have to find the extra dollars to pay for someone to fix those repairs for you. The days blend together and each night you wonder why it feels you’ve accomplished nothing, yet you’ve been running *non-stop.*

I have always said, it doesn’t matter that it’s only me living at my house, the entire yard of grass still grows! Then there is the trash. Whether it is one bag or three, there is still a container that has to be rolled to the curb every week on collection day. Meatloaf still takes an hour to bake. And oddly, furniture accumulates the same level of dust from the air! Life responsibilities are not cut in half because there is only one of me in the house now. As one person, with basically the same amount of responsibilities, it is definitely a challenge to fit in the household tasks, manage unexpected repairs, hold down our jobs, tend to our family, try to have some form of social life, and keep our sanity all at the same time.

If you are feeling overwhelmed with responsibilities, this may be a good time to re-evaluate activities and commitments that could potentially be eliminated. As much as you might love them or you might feel obligated, there comes a point where we sometimes simply have to call a stop. I used to love singing on my church's worship team. But I reached a point where I had to say, *I can't do this anymore.* It was the night I was so exhausted, I backed into my "closed" garage door as I was leaving for practice. It may be hard, but taking yourself through a realistic evaluation of your current priorities may be the first step to regaining some balance. Remember one of our self-help mantras: *I am human after all!*

Another important evaluation that will greatly reduce stress and allow you to feel more peaceful about your situation, is to ensure you process through certain types of life emergencies and create a back-up plan. I didn't have a plan early in my single life and it was challenging, to say the least. Because I had literally been married my entire adult life, I had not thought through how I would handle certain situations without a husband around. When I became separated, I merely got up the next day and launched into my life. Needless to say, that wasn't the most logical thing I could have done. I didn't think about how I would handle certain situations alone or prepare for any emergencies. *That was a mistake!*

If you've never processed through some of these thoughts or have not created a back-up plan, we're going to work on that at the end of this chapter! Doing this will be a tremendous time-saver when a problem strikes and it will allow you to remain calmer in the situation. Taking this step is so important, I have designed this book so that Chapter 8 will not open until your back-up plan is finished. That's how much I want you to be ready for the unexpected.

In case you are wondering how I accomplished that feature, I'm just kidding. Chapter 8 will open; however, the chapter is on *Faith* and you're going to need a lot of it if you don't create your back-up plan!!

I Had No Plan

When I was younger and relatively new at being single again, my car once had to go into the shop across town for a repair. You would normally think of this as a typical incident and nothing out of the ordinary. *Not so.* I don't remember how I got to work that weekday morning, yet I do remember I had not made arrangements for someone to help me pick up the car afterwards that evening. Uber was not yet available and I certainly couldn't have paid for it anyway.

When 5:00 rolled around, what did I do then? – I put my purse on my shoulder, walked down the back stairwell, and quietly slipped out the rear door of the office dressed in my skirt and heels. I proceeded to walk across our parking lot and out to the sidewalk. I then carefully and slowly walked in those heels several long blocks, nearly 2 miles, to the other side of town to get my vehicle. Thinking back on that incident now, it makes me want to cry all over again. I can remember how desperate and lonely I felt. I was in a situation with no vehicle and absolutely no one to help me.

How did that happen? Did I not work with nice people? Yes, of course I did. I simply had never had to ask for a ride before. I also worked with business people and I'm not sure any of them were even around at that hour.

Was I also too embarrassed to admit I needed help and didn't have anyone? Or did I even know how to reach out and ask. The situation was completely foreign, and I was still in that awkward new single stage. I was independent by nature and did not want to be seen as needy. I am sure there was also a part of me struggling with adjusting to being alone and it was simply easier to figure it out on my own rather than bother people every time I needed something.

Honestly, because I had not planned ahead for these situations, asking for help would have felt much more draining than that walk across town in my heels. In that moment, it was humiliating to know that I had no one. And that humiliation ran deep.

If you are recently single again and/or have not thought through these types of scenarios, please take a time-out and use my ideas to create a plan. You will save your future self from getting into a pickle of a situation or, at best, a bucket load of emotions. Even though this planning project does not sound so exciting, it will behoove you to set aside some minutes to complete it. I will give you a few starter ideas on how to make a list of your go-to people, along with a few tips I've learned along the way. *And where have I learned about these things along the way, you ask??* I'll give you 3 guesses!

At the very least in creating your plan, you will want to find a handyman or two, get the cell number of your most pleasant capable neighbor, and enlist a dependable back-up driver. Regardless of your age, health, or your currently reliable vehicle, things *are* going to happen. And they will happen when you least expect them. If you are more middle-aged, my guess is you have already had a few of these experiences. Your partner may also have been the one to handle them. If that was the case, be sure you know who was called and how to reach them.

These life scenarios could very well pop up down the road or this evening or tomorrow morning. When they strike, you will be glad you took a few moments to reflect on how you will better manage your household of one. This is a general list of ideas to help you get started. Think through your lifestyle, your particular home, things your partner may have handled for you. It is true, running a household of one can be extremely stressful, exhausting, and downright scary sometimes. Taking proactive steps, though, can minimize all of these emotions.

Creating a plan will bring you peace of mind and confidence that you can do this!

INFO

Neighbors Cell Phone #s
Save an ICE# in your cell (In Case of Emergency)
Place Emergency Contact info on a card in your wallet
Keep list of Medications and Blood Type in your wallet
Back-up Driver if you get stranded or download the Uber App
Do friends know how to reach your parents, kids, or siblings?
Keep *updated* Medical & Car Insurance Cards in your wallet
Join your neighborhood Facebook page

MEDICAL

Label a Box *Medical.* Include: Pepto, NyQuil, Cough drops, Thermometer, Cortisone, Neosporin, Ibuprofen, Band-aids
Keep Gatorade and crackers on hand *always.*
What if you throw up in the middle of the night and can't stop??

REPAIR

<u>In a convenient location, list phone numbers for:</u>
Handyman – Plumbing, Electrical, and General Repairs
Mechanic, as well as Towing Service
Your insurance company
Electric/Gas and Water Company
Critter Control
Home Warranty Company: Purchase if you own your home.
Home Warranty? #LifeSaver!

HOUSE EMERGENCIES *(Real-life-scenarios)*

What will you do if:
You wake to a soggy floor from a broken pipe?
You open your bedroom closet to water pouring on your clothes?
There's a tornado or serious thunderstorm?
A fallen tree is arcing on an electric wire in your back yard?
You see a mouse?
You hear scratching in your ceiling?
Your power goes out but it's not storming?
You come out from the grocery store and your battery is dead?

RANDOM LIFE TIPS

Change your air filters monthly.
Prioritize maintenance on your vehicle.
Purchase AAA.
Understand the oil requirement in your mower.
Learn how to fix a blown fuse.
Find your house's water shut-off and learn how to use it.
Invest in a Ring Doorbell.
Learn how to protect yourself.
Declutter so life runs smoother.
Have a good pair of work gloves and at least a basic tool set.
Create a weekly meal plan for easy grocery runs!
Get fresh air daily and purchase a good quality pillow.
Pour a full glass of water on a dark spill, then sop with a towel!
Invest in 401k. Use raises to increase your amount yearly!
Create a budget and stick to it.
Build a savings account. – Attend Ramsey's FPU!

NEXT STEPS

Something to think about...

Managing a household alone can be lonely, frustrating, exhausting, and sometimes fearful, yet those emotions focus on the negative. Consider changing your mindset to a *can-do* attitude. – Is it time to evaluate priorities??

Something to move forward...

When hardships hit around the house, it's easy to blame your past partner for leaving you in this situation. Holding anger, though, only hurts you. Who do you need to forgive? What things do you need to let go?

Something to do...

Complete your household back-up plan this week!! You have 7 days.

Ready – Set – Go!

8

Unraveling Faith

One day while sitting in my car at the beach...

Yes, *sitting in my car* at the beach, I decided I wanted to work on this specific chapter. My original plan was to be *sitting in my beach chair*, under the umbrella, listening to rolling waves, feeling the breeze, soaking in sunshine, working on this chapter at the beach. I had the perfect day mapped out. Apparently though, the radar in my weather app had a different mapping plan and those dark rain clouds I'd organized my day around did not push north over me as I was expecting. Thus, my beach plans got more than a tad thrown off-kilter even though I was there ready to enjoy my writing, a peaceful walk, and a much needed recharge.

After a few moments of sitting in my hot, dark, rain splattering SUV, trying to decide the next move, and desperately hoping for a shift in cloud cover, the sun surprisingly popped through those rain clouds. It was still raining but the sun started shining! And then

– the oddest thing. An unusual breeze stirred up and began to cool off our 96-degree heat index! Since I had made the drive out there and couldn't change the weather, I decided to enjoy what I could in the moment and make something useful of my situation until the showers passed. Squished then in my front seat, with only inches to open my laptop, these pages begin...

Even though sharing my beach experience was not the original plan for this chapter, I started to see valuable insights emerging. We'll come back to those in a few minutes. Let me start by telling you what happened as I began typing in those steaming squished inches between seat and steering wheel. I had not really been happy with this chapter's original title, so I thought I would make the most of my rainy minutes to think of a more striking chapter description while I was sitting stuck in that less-than-comfortable front seat. Thus, my brainstorming began.

The first fresh thought that surfaced was the title, "Unwavering Faith." Hmm, I wasn't sure if that phrase would fit where I wanted to go here. Nonetheless, in a true brainstorming session, you write down whatever comes to mind and then you sort it out later. So, I plunked my fingers onto my laptop's keyboard. Mind you, I generally type really well. (It comes in handy when you decide you want to write a book!) However, when you're cramped between a steering wheel, a sun glazed computer screen, and 96 humid degrees, all bets are off on the typing accuracy. I looked down and discovered I was actually typing, u n **r** a v... Ohhh, hmm, wrong letter... yet wait. This can be a word, too! Another brainstorm in the middle of the current brainstorm! And so I finished – *Unraveling* Faith. Could that work? Does it fit? Shift-F7.

> Thesaurus: Unscrambling. Straightening Out. Untangling.
> – *Failing. Crumbling. Falling to pieces.*

Wow, yes! If *unraveling* does not describe our faith sometimes living as a single, I don't know what does. I love it. Brainstorm over. Chapter title accomplished.

"Unraveling"

There was also something quite interesting that popped to my attention as I was glancing over the options for this word. *Unraveling* contains two completely polar meanings within itself! (I'm not sure I ever fully thought that a word could do that.) As I glanced over my thesaurus suggestions, I saw where 'unraveling' can have a negative slant. – To mean a feeling of crumbling or falling to pieces. "With the frustration of my situation, I feel like my faith is unraveling." However, 'unraveling' also carries an uplifting, *positive* meaning, as well! – Unscrambling. Untangling. "I have been in quite the mess with my faith recently, but I'm committed to unraveling it!"

At the risk of sounding a bit on the nerdy side, I have to say I did get a pinch excited about this. – With all you have going on in your world, at this moment you may be feeling quite *unraveled* (crumbled, collapsed) in your faith. If you are experiencing these emotions, I'm hoping we can work to *unravel* (untangle, work out) those feelings of your situation to help strengthen your faith! This double-sided word perfectly expresses what I hope we can accomplish in these pages: Working together through the unraveling of your life so that you might live, *unraveled!*

It is my genuine prayer that, as we talk through this faith subject, you will find greater hope, comfort, and peace in your life, especially through your single again journey. Whether you are barely hanging on by a thread, or you're not sure you have ever experienced true faith in the past, or you think this topic is not for you, please stick with me here. – In case you haven't yet noticed, I was not exactly graced with the sweet-little-church-lady gene. In these pages, you are not going to hear any syrupy sermons speaking from these fingertips. As we walk through this chapter, I will keep our conversation real, genuine, and down-to-earth. No guilt trips here; this section is designed to encourage you, right where you are, bumps and all.

To shed some light on why *faith*, why I want you to stick with me through this chapter, I'd like to share a bit of my background. It's important for me that you understand I am coming to you from a very human perspective. Very imperfect. Quite honestly, while I have developed an incredibly deep faith in my life, I am oddly awkward trying to talk about it. I do know it's an extremely important piece for you though in your single journey, and so I will try in my limited ability to strongly encourage you to include God in your life. Not God in the sense of *religion*, I am encouraging you to have a *relationship* with God. In spite of all my mishaps, my own unraveling, I am ever so grateful for my faith and the relationship I have with him. I do not want to live a single breath of my life without God in it. That said, I did not arrive to this place easily.

God Takes Us as We Are

Below is a snippet of how my world began and how I reached the secure place where I now reside. I've not shared a lot of detail about my early background, so let me give you the *very* high level summary. I want you to see that, if I can get to this faith place, you can, too. It should take all of about two sentences to paint this picture.

Growing up, I was raised in a relatively strict protestant church, as well as a rather nice home, in a rather nice subdivision, in which I was taught to be ladylike, smart, and to conduct myself appropriately in public. Okay, there you have it. That only took one sentence! Can you picture it? Easter Sunday morning. Age 4. Sitting on the hearth of the fireplace in my light pleated skirt suit, white patent leather shoes, my hair lifted into an adorable bun with its velvet bow, and of course the white gloves. You see me in the home movies, gently waving like a princess into the lens of my dad's movie camera, while my two older brothers sit beside me in their new suits, pressed shirts, and bow ties.

As I grew and when I was not dressed and presenting myself for a special occasion, you would find us playing with the neighbors around our hilltop cul-de-sac. And what were we playing? Sometimes it was the typical hide-n-seek on a summer night. During the day though? I mostly remember playing school or *business*! Yes, you read that right. We turned the top of our circle into a small city, complete with chalk-drawn divider stripes on the street, shops, a restaurant, and a bank. When I was not playing with the neighbor kids, my world consisted of homework, good grades, cheerleading, church on Sunday morning, and youth group Sunday night. Thus, I enter adult life with the most appropriately trained upbringing.

As you can imagine, divorce was not really acceptable in my world, much less living years as a single woman rather than jumping back into a traditional marriage. Additionally, I have always felt I have a somewhat independent, passionate nature which has left me feeling different from the other ladies in my world. In the many years following my divorce, I was an odd combination of my prim and proper upbringing, this spirited personality, and living decades as an independent, full-of-life, strong-willed, single person. Yet all the while never truly disowning my roots. I was an unraveled ball of conflicting emotion and faith experience. Having a well trained foundation, yet struggling. Wishing I could be sweet-natured like I was taught, yet possessing such a strong will. Truly loving God (most of the time), yet wondering how the God-relationship fit into my whirlwind less-than-perfect, single life.

And guess what? It took some years, yet I can now genuinely say, *it's okay. I'm* okay! With all of my imperfections, mistakes, and personality traits, I am still just fine, as I am. While Grace is not my middle name, I know now that God created me with this specific personality. On purpose. He's the one who precisely designed my character traits. He knows me and he can manage me. Every single quirk of my being.

I also know he did the same for you. Wherever you are, whoever you've become, whatever path you may be walking, however angry or frustrated you might be, whatever doubts you may have, however much you may have pushed him away... God is there. He created you. He designed you. He *knows* you. And he wants you. Not through some guilt-ridden religion. He wants you in pure, human form, as-you-are, relationship.

If you doubt this about yourself, find your bible and read Psalm 139. (If you don't have a bible, you can pull it up online or visit your local bookstore.) Wherever you can get your hands on a bible, open to the middle and find the book of Psalms. Then saturate yourself in Psalm 139. You are not alone. Not a lost cause. God is still with you in whatever unraveling state you might currently find yourself.

> **If you ever feel you have strayed too far or failed too much, I can clearly say, NO YOU HAVEN'T!**

God is always there ready to wrap his arms around you, forgive you, love you, bless you, and sustain you in this journey regardless of how far off course you've gone. I have walked many many miles down the single life path. And sometimes that path was winding.

After my marriage and several dating attempts, I have been single again, and single again, and *single again* to the point where it seemed like there was no hope for anything good in my life. And of course there were times, probably more than I want to remember, where God got the blame for it. While I don't like to admit, I have definitely had my moments with God. I reached places where I wondered what was the point of having faith. I've cried. Actually I've *screamed* at God, being transparent here. I've had times where I've questioned why. Times where life made no sense. Where I did *not* understand. Where I felt hopeless. I've been angry with God. Boldly voiced my disapproval. I have veered off course. Made mistakes. I've felt unworthy. Name an emotion. I've been there... and so was he.

Through every situation and season, I have come to realize one core truth. *God has been there in every moment with me.* When I didn't understand the why of a situation, he gave me the ability to trust and grow through it. In the exhausted moments when I felt as though I could sink, I did not. When I thought I was going to go under financially, I did not. When I thought I could not hurt any more deeply, I was comforted. When I thought I was not worthy to ever do good for God again, he opened opportunity.

Even with my not so warm 'n fuzzy personality, God has allowed me to have confidence that I have worth and I am not a lost cause. Not only has he reassured me he can work with my quirks, he reminds me over and over again that HE is the one who designed my being and HE is the one who orchestrates my paths. Wherever you are, whoever you are, God knows where you've slipped and he is there when you're ready to step closer.

Maybe you've not ever had a relationship with God. Possibly in your circumstances your faith is quite unraveled right now. Or you may be so hurt you've simply grown cold to the idea. Wherever you find yourself, I strongly encourage you to consider entering into (or back into) a close relationship with him. There is such an underlying peace and confidence that has carried me through the toughest of times, I cannot imagine surviving without God in my life.

I want that same peace for you. If this is a foreign concept to you or you have no idea how someone has a relationship with God, that's okay, too. I'll give some down to earth guidance in a few pages. For now, keep hanging with me. There is one more sensitive area I want to address first. – That question which can easily run rampant in the mind of a single.

But God, Why?!

Oh, if this isn't the age old question! "If God is so loving, why did He allow .....?" "If God cares so much about me, why haven't I found someone?" "If a relationship with God is so great, where was He when I ......?" Fill in the blank.

I want to address this. Please note, I am not addressing with some lofty theological answer. I'm simply addressing with the good human common sense God gave me, because that is one character trait for which I *am* grateful!

The question then: If God is so great, loving, and capable, why did that horrible experience happen to me? As gently as I can say this... Things happen because we are living in life and, well, things are still going to happen. It's not so much about *what* happens, rather how God works through us *when* they do happen. A life lived with God is simply LIFE lived *with* God. We've entered into **life** with him, not a candy store! Does God bless sometimes in amazingly miraculous ways? Yes, He certainly does! But does this solely define the meaning or basis of life with God? Not at all!

Think of it this way... You have a great friend. Sometimes that friend surprises you with a wonderful gift. Or sometimes you might ask that friend for a favor and they gladly jump in to help when they can. While this is part of a good friendship, is this the only reason you have that person as a friend? Of course not! That friendship is there because you spend time with each other, you enjoy doing things together, you have respect, you support each other in the bad times. While this is only a snippet, this is somewhat similar to having a relationship with God. Receiving only goodness from this day forward quite honestly doesn't make any sense!

We are living human life and thus, human things are going to happen. If I eat too much sugar, I'm going to get a belly ache. That's just the nature of the human body. On a more serious note, sometimes sickness or accidents happen to us because we are living the human life. When these things happen or seem to happen to an extreme, it does sometimes feel like "God is not being fair" or that we got dealt a bad hand. I can't say I completely understand why it does seem that way. I do believe though, that good can come from even the worst of times. God enables us to leverage those situations to encourage others walking in similar shoes. Our adversity then becomes a blessing.

Do you not think I could be bitter or angry because God allowed me to be single for such a long time? I suppose I could take that approach. Instead, I simply thought it might be better to trust God had his reasons. He orchestrated my circumstances to have me presently *exactly* where He wants me. I then have made the choice to take those decades of my single-again experience and share it with you in hopes that I might encourage you in your single-again experience!

To me, THIS is part of the meaning of having life with God. Not spoiled with life being handed to me on a silver platter. Rather, having peace when the platter drops and shatters at my feet into a million pieces. Honestly, I don't want to be the spoiled child with all of life handed to me. Where is the character in that? How does that make me a better person??

Moving Forward

If you are angry or frustrated with God or blaming him for allowing something extremely hurtful in your life, I am going to encourage you to put the situation in your past and then, either leave it there or, leverage it to help others. I want to ask you to trust God. Let that situation go and *move forward*. Your mental health, your physical health, and the direction of your future depends on it!

God allows people to make their own choices in life and that, unfortunately, means sometimes we will randomly get caught in the awful consequences of those choices. I know it is easy to blame God. It's easy to stay angry or seek revenge. I have been at the edge of that cliff! Then, I've had to face the reality that some things are beyond my control and I have to trust God's reason for allowing it. There is a tipping point where the anger and energy invested in the bitterness end up only hurting one person. Yourself. If it was a hurt you endured, whatever someone did to you, accept that it happened, then take back your joy and *your life*! That person is unworthy of your peace and happiness. Brush your hands of them and watch what God has in store for you.

Hello God

If you think you have been away from God too long or you have made too many mistakes, the simple answer to that is – *No*, you haven't. If you have stepped away, become preoccupied with life, or gotten mixed up in unhealthy relationships, simply come back. God is here. Patiently and lovingly waiting to restore you.

If you have no idea where to begin or how to even "talk" to God, here are some pointers to get you started:

First, you'll want to start by having a conversation with God. Be yourself. God isn't going to expect you to sound like a pro. (Quite frankly, Jesus mentioned he doesn't even like that!) If you truly do not know what you should say, I can help. If it were me – and I do unfortunately have experience at this – my conversation would sound something like this:

"God.... [long pause]. I don't even know where to begin. I probably don't deserve this, and I'm going to ask anyway... My world is upside down... and I'm empty... and I know I've let life get in the way. The reality is, I want you in my life. I am truly sorry I got so sidetracked. (Feel free to confess and elaborate here.) Please let me start over. I do trust you with my life. I trust your reasons for all that has happened. And I trust YOU with my future – even though I don't see it right now. Starting at this moment, I do want to live every day of my life with you in it."

Note: I purposely simplified here to get you started, and the Next Steps will help you successfully continue.

If this is a new turn in life for you, fasten your seat belt. Life just got better! Not perfect. *Better*. Richer. More meaningful. Purposeful. Sweeter. Every day of your life.

Lessons from the Beach Day

I sat crunched in my SUV on the beach that day, trying to make the most of my dreadful rainy situation. I was disappointed. That rain was unexpected and it ruined everything I had planned. I had my writing objectives for the day. I physically needed the recharge of a walk and to breathe fresh air into my lungs. I wanted my body to absorb vitamin D from the sunshine. I had checked the weather and had it all specifically planned out in a way that would allow me to get energized in order to stay on task with my specific book goals. I had done all the right things to have my day set in order and, just as I arrived, my day turned upside down.

Does this sound familiar? Do we not also have our lives planned out? Goals. Needs. Down times to catch our breath. Plans for the future. I saw my life in that experience on the beach. I had made all the right plans and then, without warning, clouds formed. Not the fun white puffy clouds where you see the jumping poodle or the woolly sheep. Black clouds. Thick and heavy. The kind that you know are about to pour. In the south, I've heard them say, "The bottom's about to fall out."

> That is the description of what happens sometimes in our life. Those times. *These* times, perhaps? The rains have come. Unexpected. Unwanted. The bottom has fallen out.

Just as the weather rolled in that day and unraveled my plans, the storms of life can swiftly roll in and unravel our faith. Your spouse announces they want to leave. A new relationship turns south. There's another person. Your life partner unexpectedly dies. This was not your plan. Where is God in all of this? The bills mount. Kids are impacted. Friendships change. *This is God's plan?* The stress adds up. Maintaining your home. Needing support yet having none. Wanting a break. Needing to breathe. Suffocating. 96 degree heat index. How do I trust in God with this??

And then, sitting there crunched in the front seat of my steaming car, trying to stay positive, little things began to happen.

First, I suddenly realized the rain was coming down in a very unique direction. Oddly, I was able to put my windows completely down. I was able to take in deep breaths of the gulf air and I wasn't getting wet! Then, I felt a *cool* breeze blow in from outside! If you have ever been to the gulf coast in the middle of summer, you know that the words "cool" and "breeze" are never found in the same sentence. What was happening?! I'm not sure what was happening, but it was so refreshing and energizing – and a little bit on the exciting side. I had never had this experience before, *nor was it natural*. Next, after a brief shower, those horrible thick clouds parted right over the area where I was parked. It was completely ugly all around, but the ugly parted and the most radiant circle of sunshine and bright blue skies poured over me.

As I sat there, trying to concentrate on how I would find the words to talk about "unraveling" our faith, there was a supernatural faith story unraveling before my eyes. You see, this is exactly how it works when we decide to trust God and his purpose in our lives. When we feel we are suffocating in the heat of our situation, if we let down the window, he will bring his spirit, his supernatural *cool breeze* to refresh us. When it feels like there is nothing but dark clouds with no light in sight for our life, he is still there. While for a moment I couldn't see that beautiful sunshine, it was there all the time. And when we have our moments where it appears God is not there, he is. He can pull back the darkness and shine his beautiful warmth and light to encourage you right there in the middle of your storm. And that rain you see pouring around you? God is fully capable to shift the winds of your circumstances so that you can let go and the rain won't touch you.

Before my disruptive day on the beach, I was feeling a bit unraveled on how to write this chapter. While I didn't plan for rain that day and certainly didn't want it, that unexpected storm was the catalyst that actually *freed* my mind and helped me form the words I'd so struggled to find. Rain on a beach day is not ever anything you look forward to, yet it was the rain experience that allowed God to work best with my goals. Not only did I get to finish my chapter in spite of the messy weather, I also came away with life lessons and a renewed enthusiasm for the way God works in the worst of circumstances!

Do you feel like you are living right now under heavy clouds? Is it downright pouring in your life or has the darkness allowed your faith to simply unravel? I encourage you to keep going, trust God, and look up. Watch the rain shift. Feel the spirit of God send a fresh breath into the middle of your circumstances. Be amazed and experience the supernatural unraveling he is about to bring in your faith and on your life!

NEXT STEPS

Something to think about...

Is your focus so much on the storms that it has allowed your faith to become somewhat unraveled? (How's that working for you??)

Something to move forward...

Let's start with the bible. Whether online or from a book store, the book of John in the New Testament is a good beginning. Even though you're busy, find a few moments every day to read and check in with God.

Something to do...

Okay, this is potentially going to be challenging. I said life would be better, not easier! Do a little research and, this next Sunday, start the process of finding a church that fits your style. (If you are currently involved in a church where you have single friendships, that's awesome. Most of us can't say we have that.)

Having friends who also have God in their life is like a cool breeze in summer on the gulf coast.

9

We Should Have Dinner Sometime

Ummm, is this a date???
Seriously... I don't know.
I do know we're friends. Are we *that* kind of friends??
The way you asked... I just thought maybe this was...

Ohh, I have had those moments. Those dinners, the invitations. Have you experienced them yet? If you haven't, hold on because you likely will! When you least expect it. When you *don't* expect it. Those friendships that develop and one day you're not sure if it's intended to be more than what it is. Not that I minded with some. Although some I did mind because they put me in an awkward position. Whew, the topic of attraction and dating! Yi-yi-yi.

> Even if you think you don't want to date, don't plan to date, or don't like to date. Read on. Thank me later.

Dating invitations can sneak up on you when you least expect them. Ready or not. Wanted or not. They'll pop out of the blue from a long-time friend, or a guy you barely know in your social group, a friend of a friend, an awkward work colleague, or even someone extending an invitation while standing in the grocery aisle! (Yes, true story.) Then, what do you do with them?! Okay, the grocery store guy, pretty easy to laugh him off. The others, though??

It might be good to create a response plan! Whether you have dating intentions or not, these invitations can surface from the most unlikely (and sometimes unwanted) places. Wherever you are with this topic, feel free to peruse these next pages and chapters. I've personally never been completely comfortable with dating, so I have a few rather real-life stories for you. Laugh. Cringe. Cry with me. Think. Plan. Get ready. *Your time* may be just around the corner!

Not Exactly a *Dinner* Request

After my divorce, I was not at all ready for the situations I was about to encounter. I'd been married a long time and had no single friends, so I was neither prepped nor practiced as I embarked on this new journey. – If there was ever a time I wish I could have pulled out an Instruction Manual, *this* would have been the time!

With no manual, then, I entered single life. And I learned. I learned that invitations come not only *when* you least expect, they also may come in *forms* you least expect! I learned that, in the single life, there is dating. There is having a date. Then there are those moments when someone, without invitation, simply wants to *Go Directly to Jail and Not Pass Go!* You hear about these things, but you certainly think they only happen to other people. Let me confirm, sometimes they don't.

Right out of the gate, I was initiated with my first bizarre experience. Quite shortly after my divorce was finalized, someone I knew well, a very married family man, slipped me a note one day at work. I don't remember the detail. What I do remember, he was basically making himself *available*. Ewww. That's all I have to say. Just *ewww*, and no! What?! I'm not sure the ink was even dry on my divorce papers. Where in the world did that come from? And thank you for making it awkward now that I have to be around you.

Being the bigger person, I politely declined and went on my way *in the opposite direction!* Wow, let the learning begin. Lesson #1: Bizarre invitations might happen – and from people you least expect. I knew this person, but certainly not in that way!

Dinner with a *Friend?*

I wish I could say that interaction was the only awkward moment I was forced to maneuver through my single years. The reality? Friendships with the opposite sex can sometimes get misunderstood. Where one may be reserved and never make that move you wish for, another will completely misinterpret your friendliness. Once, after two months of alleged dinner dates, I had to ask a guy if he was ever going to kiss me! On the flip side, there was the time I had a friend who one day announced he couldn't take it anymore and, before I could ask, "*Take what?*", he swooped me up in his arms! – Okay, didn't see that one coming.

Or you might have an encounter like one of my friends who lived up north. The country was experiencing heavy snow storms and, in the middle of a chat one afternoon, she stopped and said, "Oh, hang on a sec." – It was her mechanic texting. (Her recently divorced mechanic, I might add.) He was wanting to know if she'd like him to come over and plow her driveway. *Yehh,* right.

Then there was the great guy friend who called me at an ungodly hour one night asking if he could come over and talk. I'm a good friend, so of course I was okay with him needing to talk. I really thought nothing of it. After he arrived, I found out he wanted to talk about dating me! He was the coolest friend ever, but *no*, we weren't compatible in that way. Seriously? You came over at this hour to discuss that?!

Or you will have the long-time friend who you think may be more than a friend, but you don't say anything. And neither does he. Only for you to learn years later, at one of those crossroads, he had had feelings for you. But life went on... and changed... and so did your paths. *Oh the predicaments and decisions of boy meets girl.*

While some situations can be a little more unique than others, some *will* be genuine invitations for a date to dinner. To accept or not to accept then, that will be the question. Do you step out and say yes? Is there ever an easy way around our decision to take the risk on a new relationship? Is this the chapter where I break out the magic formula to make all of this much easier for you?

I will definitely help you navigate; however, there can be no magic manual. Friendships and attractions are all unique. We each bring our individual personalities, desires, range of experiences, and our current places in life which influence our decisions where we decide. To ask. Or to refrain. To say not right now. Or to say, *No, I'm good...* And sometimes, to say, *Yes!*

Yes, *But...*

If you are slightly unsure of yourself or feel shy about saying yes. If you don't feel prepared for a dating relationship. If you have fear about even going on a date. – *You are not alone!*

I know you're not alone, because these phrases describe thoughts I've heard from others and thoughts I've had myself. For most of my years, I genuinely disliked dating. Regardless of how interested in someone I might feel, there was a host of reservations I experienced. Insecurity, fear, sadness, and uncertainty were just a few of the emotions holding me back.

Let me address sadness first. It is a very real and valid emotion, and it is okay if you are feeling sad about moving on with someone new. A while after my divorce, I eventually dated someone quite seriously for over two years, and then I went through a heartbreaking ending of that relationship.

At that time, I was involved with a singles group and eventually there was a nice guy from the group who asked me to the movies. There was really no reason to say no, other than it made me sad to be going to the movies with someone else and not *my movie partner*. When the evening arrived, there was a pit in my stomach which started on my way home from work. I couldn't face going to the movies with someone else, and the tears began to well up. Within minutes they were rolling down my face and continued the entire time I was trying to get dressed. By the time the guy pulled into my driveway, I had barely dried my face and replaced the streaks of mascara down my cheeks. But I did it. And guess what? I actually had a really good time and he could not have been nicer. We eventually stopped dating, only because I was at a different place in my life with grown kids and his were younger. But that first date turned out to be OKAY, and I'm glad I pushed myself to accept the invitation.

Beyond stepping out and accepting that *first date* after my breakup, dating in general carried its own basket of anxieties for me. Looking back and seeing the reasons spelled out here, they do appear rather trivial. In my mind, however, the angst was real.

And so I begin… First of all, I have NOTHING to wear!! In my day world, I worked a business job. Thus, I had a closet full of business clothes. I never felt I had the right social outfits to go on a date. You know that scene in movies where the woman is holding up dress after dress trying to decide which to wear? That's real life! Well, minus the cute dresses.

I have no cute dresses. That part is not real life, at least not in my closet! But outfit choice after outfit choice? Yes. Add multiple top/bottom combinations. Strewn across the bed. On the body. Off the body. Clock ticking. Anxiety rising. Self-talk escalating. Then it hits rock bottom. *I can't do this!!* And then tears. And then the downward spiral of conversation with myself. *I can't date.* I can't afford this. *I never should have accepted.* More tears. Then the feeling of being absolutely trapped in my single life because I merely can't find an outfit for a simple date. You know – If you can't go out on a date, you will never find a partner and, without a partner, you are destined to be alone!

Yes, I'm aware that sounds a bit melodramatic, so I pull in my quivering bottom lip. Eventually, the outfit comes together. The face gets washed. The make-up gets reapplied. The date begins. It's a fun time and I quickly discover there was all the fuss for nothing. – Until the check comes for dinner.

Traditionally, if a man asks you on a date, it's expected he'll pay. That's very kind for a first date. But what if I didn't have a great time and I know I don't want to go out with him again? Is it horrible to let him pay? If he pays, is there some type of expectation? An expectation for another date? Or at the end of the night?? What if I offer to pay? Is that an insult? And do I really have the money anyway? Then, if I think I would like to go out again, who pays the next time? Or the next? That doesn't seem fair yet my budget does not allow for big dinners out. Thus, a new turmoil develops.

Alas, after a few dates, I learn there are alternatives to paying for dates. Again the quivering lip pulls in and all it well. Going to the movies? Offer to buy the popcorn. Bonus, join AMC Stubs! Not only do you get to skip the long food line, you also get a free upsize on drinks! There are ways to contribute to a dating relationship on a shoestring budget.

Also, before you feel too guilty about letting him pay for the date, consider what you're spending on those new outfits you've had to purchase! Honestly, I've been to special events where I know the cost of my clothing was more than the price of the event. Dry your tears. Pull in your quivering lip. Get creative and date guilt-free. Besides, if he doesn't like the expense, he can get budget creative, too!

So you settle into the idea of trying a few more dates together. Conversation is comfortable, you have things in common, and you enjoy having their company. Now comes that awkward stage. Yes, that one – the point when you're wondering if it's appropriate to show or respond to affection. Are you on the same page as them? Is it moving too fast? Too slow? Are they too touchy in public? Or maybe you've discovered they have *verrry* different levels of intimacy expectations and beliefs. I wish so much I could tell you there's a formula and, if you follow it, you'll have a wonderful mutual experience in the romance department. I'm not even going to Google that one. I know that every situation is different. Every person's history, set of values, affection style, and level of attraction is unique. There is probably only one thing we all have in common: Most of us will have at least one crazy story we can look back on later to laugh about!

Oops

While a lot of dating experiences go as planned, some of them, well, *don't* go as planned. Sometimes you discover it in the first meeting; sometimes it's a few dates later. I once enjoyed someone's company for several weeks thinking we were very similar, and then discovered he lived in quite the unkempt house. (Which is *not* very similar to me, at all!) Other times, I've had dates exaggerate their height, and I mean exaggerate their height! I've even had older men provide a completely younger age to me. Stay tuned! Some of these made it into my Chapter 10 Bloopers. *Is it any wonder my hairstylist used to say she lived vicariously through me?!* Oh the stories I could tell and the fun we would have at those hair appointments.

While saying yes to a date (or two or three) may not turn out to be quite what you expected, it can also turn out exciting and fun. Those initial fears can give way to butterflies in your stomach and a rewarding relationship. When you say, *yes*, just remember to take it one date at a time and enjoy the discovery. If it doesn't work, the best thing you can do is learn from the experience and move on. Can it be frustrating or sad? Sometimes yes, but not always. When it doesn't work out, simply take your 5 minutes to vent or cry, accept that things happen, and look forward to new dating adventures in the future. Realistically, will some experiences require more than a 5-minute cry? Yes, this happens. We'll dig a little deeper on that topic in Chapter 13.

Platonic Relationships

There will be other times along your single journey when you find yourself in a space where dating is shelved for a while. During these times, you may have at least one male friend who fills the gap for you in the companion department making your life feel comfortable and content. Yes, that good friend-of-the-opposite-sex who is "just a friend." – Platonic.

I don't have a sole chapter for this topic, and I probably should. While platonic relationships make wonderful friends, there could (and likely will) come a time when one of you may consider crossing the line beyond just the friendship. I mean, what better person to date than someone who knows you with all your bumps – and probably without makeup! Right? Well, not so fast.

Some words of caution on this subject: First, be mindful of the way the two of you interact. If, in time, you notice the other person becoming a little more friendly, affectionate, or flirtatious with you, this could be a signal that deeper feelings are developing on their part. These little changes might be revealing that your friend is beginning to see you as more than just a friend. If you do notice shifts in behavior, be cautious about playing into the flirtation. You won't want to lead them on if you know you don't have a romantic interest. This can be hurtful to both your friend and the friendship, itself.

If you do decide to move from only friendship into a dating relationship, be mindful of the possible outcome. If it doesn't work out, you may end up losing a good friend. Once that line has been crossed, it's a challenge to go back to the way things were.

While it's great company to have a friend of the opposite sex, understand it has the potential to get tricky. There may be a bridge for you to cross in the distance! It's best to have this possibility tucked in the back of your head so you're ready for the conversation... *or decision.* 'Better to consider the possibility and be ready rather than fumble when it happens and you lose a dear friend.

The Top Ten List

You might consider one of your male friends *just a friend* because they don't exactly measure up to what you're looking for in a romantic relationship. Have you considered that? Have you ever specifically created a "Top 10 List" of character traits you would like to have in a partner? I did once. Oddly, I was recently clearing old boxes and found my original list! It was so priceless, I tucked it away in my box of humorous memories.

Back in the day I was adamant about following my list. It's funny to think back on it now. It actually never occurred to me – such a man may not even exist on this earth! Nor did the possibility occur to me that, if he did exist, I may not meet *his* Top 10 list of desired traits! At the time, though, it made perfect sense and I was determined to find my description of a man. Mind you, I was younger and quite full of energy when it came to thinking about what I specifically wanted in a partner. If a man didn't check all my boxes, I could quickly check *him* off my list of potential beaus.

The danger in being so rigid with your expectations, however, is that it can cause you to miss out on a potentially loving relationship. I had the special opportunity once to date someone who had great qualities and was quite financially stable. He absolutely adored me and wanted to marry me. I also cared for him deeply. Why did I turn him down, then?? Well, there were boxes unchecked. One of them was I didn't think we had enough in common. Item #6, *Must love football!* I remember telling my friends, "I don't know. He likes tennis and I like football. Also, I like going to movies and he would rather watch movies at home." To which my friends replied, "Michelle, with that kind of money, you can build your *own* theater!" Nonetheless, I couldn't get past my list and, in the end, I stuck to my decision. We did remain friends for many many years but, sadly, he never remarried.

Your list should keep you level-headed, not paralyzed!

I agree, it's silly to think you can create a Top 10 List and your perfect match-of-a-being will one day step into your beautiful mold. There is, however, some positive that comes from stating the qualities you would like in a life partner! Even if you plan to steer clear of dating for now, I strongly encourage you to at least create a list for yourself. It gives you a framework and provides a guide for you when considering a new relationship.

Speaking of creating a *Date Guide*, to this point we've been evaluating invitations which come from someone you know in person. However, with dating apps, social media, and long distance potential, this brings a completely different perspective to creating a list of "must-haves" for venturing into a new relationship! Hold on to that thought. These topics are coming in the next chapters.

Remember, if you think any of these scenarios would never apply to you, life has a way of throwing curve balls when you least expect them! Having a plan and creating your list will definitely help you clarify your core non-negotiables. Those listed goals can keep you levelheaded when someone unexpectedly enters your life and the butterflies begin to cloud your vision (and your good common sense). Believe me, it happens!

As you consider the traits you would like to see in a partner, consider also the traits you would like to see in the *relationship!* (My original list had none of those and it was a big miss.) Allow this framework to be your guide. Then, remember to review and evaluate often. Where once upon a time, I loved going to the theater, I now much rather enjoy Netflix with a bowl of popcorn curled up on the recliner with my favorite squishy blanket!... I've also learned that having a man interested in taking me to football games is not nearly as satisfying if he doesn't hold my hand.

Process and visualize your list. What does it look like?? Then, look again! What details are missing and what is making you feel special in each of those lines? What can you live without? And what can you *not* live without? Then once you have your framework, remember, no one will fit it perfectly. Be flexible. Use it as a *guide*.

After you begin dating someone, I encourage you to revisit your list. When we get in a routine and it becomes comfortable, it is oddly very easy to accept parts of a relationship that are not so enjoyable for us. If we aren't careful, we can even overlook aspects of a relationship that are borderline unhealthy emotionally. Without being overly rigid about your top tens, you still want to ensure you are staying true to your desires and especially your values. You deserve to be happy. You deserve to have someone compatible. And you deserve to be respected and loved. Of course flexibility is a part of every relationship. But compromise of your core desires? No.

Picking Daisies

After saying that initial *yes* to a date and accepting more dates, you will reach a point where you can say you are officially *dating*! As time passes, you'll begin to notice your feelings are developing for them. But do they feel the same about you??

Remember that game when we were kids? He loves me. He loves me not. Did you ever play this roulette flower game with your heart and a fresh daisy when you were young?! I have no idea whoever taught me this trick. Ha, probably my mom, but I actually believed it. Pluck out a petal and say, *He loves me.* Pluck out another, *He loves me not.* Pluck. Repeat. Pluck. Repeat. On the last petal, you have your answer!

Okay, I was TEN, and I did not carry the practice into adulthood. At least not with a daisy. I have, though, in a dating relationship found myself reaching a point where I wanted to know how someone felt. In my mind, I was probably subconsciously repeating *he loves me, he loves me not*, yet I always feared breaching the subject. Some people don't fall easily and it can be months, if ever, that you will hear those words. Others may fall more quickly and speak the words before you are ready. Keep in mind, either way does not make one person right or wrong, it is merely how a person feels... and they simply might not be on the same page as you.

You may likely find yourself in one of these situations, and that's okay. Either way, I encourage you to keep a pulse on your feelings and be prepared to respond. If your partner speaks those words and you are not there yet with your emotions, you might consider reinforcing how much you care for them and explain you are slower in relationships. On the other hand, if you feel you are in a relationship which is not progressing as deeply as you'd like, find a time to talk about it. While it may be hurtful, it is better for you to find out sooner than later if you are dating someone who does not see you in a romantically, loving way. More than anything, be honest with yourself. In the long run, honesty is truly the best thing for you.

The Next Chapter

Regardless of how you have come to be single, there will come a new day when someone will ask you to dinner again. The invitation might make you feel hesitant, nervous, anxious, sad, or guilty, or a host of other emotions. *That is okay!* Start yourself a new chapter. Take a deep breath and go have a good time!

NEXT STEPS

Something to think about...

What emotions surface when you think about dating?

Something to move forward...

Close your eyes and picture your last relationship as a chapter in a book coming to a close. Take a deep breath. Now, relax as you turn the page and visualize a new chapter beginning.

Something to do...

Create your Top Ten List. Be sure to add traits you desire in the person, *as well as* traits you desire in the relationship!

Dating is a risk. Companionship is its reward.

10

What Does it Mean to Swipe Right?

And then there is online dating...

Wait. Resist the urge to skip this chapter. If the phrase "online dating" causes a shiver to run through your spine and your head to shake on a swivel, stay with me! You may think this form of dating is absolutely not for you. There may be stories from friends or worse yet, horror stories surfacing from the recesses of your mind. You may still have scars from a recent burn. You are too old to do something like this. Yes, Yes, Yes, and Yes. I check *all* those boxes! Again, I encourage you to stay with me here.

This is truly a section to guide you through online dating; however, most of the principles will apply in general when meeting someone new, tips on evaluating compatibility, and more. Even if you have no interest or foreseeable opportunity in front of you, it is good (and wise) to be prepared. When you least expect it, there is going to be that friend suddenly introduce you to someone. Or... One day you may decide to test the virtual waters.

A while after my divorce, I had ventured onto the internet, more out of curiosity than anything else. I have to agree, there was not a plethora of suitable matches; however, I actually met some truly nice men through that avenue. One of those nice men even became one of my dearest friends. He didn't live in my area and we became friends merely through talking. It was seven years before we ever met in person. Through all our years we were great sounding boards for each other providing a mutual safe place to talk about life and our dating woes between relationships. We offered each other valuable perspectives about the opposite sex, and I wouldn't trade those years of friendship for the world.

While I did have my fair share of drastic internet stories, I refused to allow those people to keep me from having other healthy and meaningful friendships. In time, however, my career picked up and I ventured my way into a long term relationship, thus, I closed my first chapters of internet dating.

Emmanuel

More years passed. Then life shifted. My long term relationship ended and I once again found myself labeled in single status. During that period, I had a position where I traveled a bit for work. One benefit of business travel is that your hotel staff gets to know you, and they look forward to catching up each time you visit! At least mine did.

Or maybe we caught up with each other because they kept the Bistro open past 10pm to accommodate my ridiculously long work hours. Nonetheless, it was wonderful to have good company and dinner after a long work day on the road. Most nights Emmanuel would see me coming and start fixing my usual. Caesar salad, add grilled chicken, Caesar on the side.

Unbeknownst to me, that kind young man had also been keeping tabs on my unhappy relationship through those ending months. He even knew the week I was planning to make a decision about my unhealthy relationship and was looking forward to hearing the story on my next trip!

After recapping the tale of my baffling breakup, Emmanuel of course wanted to stick up for me and had a plan ready to get me back in the swing of things. Although, I wasn't exactly looking for a plan, it made me smile to have the support of a young person looking out for me. The suggestion, though? You can imagine. He suggested I get on *Tinder*. Whoa! I was not all that experienced in the world; however, I had heard stories. Tinder was known as a hook-up site. (I had to learn what that term meant, as well. When you're older and in a long-term relationship, some of these words are simply not part of your everyday vocabulary.) Needless to say, I had heard enough along my journeys to know I was NOT the kind of girl to be on Tinder! Well, Emmanuel reassured me this dating site had cleaned up its reputation and he did his best to convince me there were a lot of "*really nice people on there.*" I enjoyed the banter, needed the good laugh, and cut a deal with Emmanuel: If I tried it and ended up marrying someone from Tinder, I promised to invite him to the wedding! (Ha, I'm laughing remembering back on our conversation.)

The Online Adventure

Mind you, it had been nearly a decade since I had ventured into any type of dating site. Nonetheless, Emmanuel had convinced me enough that this one was safe and I might meet someone nice. At some point later then, I decided to check it out. I have no idea how I searched and found Tinder, although I do recall I found it using my cell phone. I did not comprehend that it was an "app" rather than a "site"...and I obviously thought it would operate similar to the standard dating platforms from my past. I filled out the brief bio info they requested and was ready to roll! Except it did not take me on the familiar route I had remembered from my past.

Once I hit the *Submit* button, the only thing on my screen was a photo. A photo. Just a photo! Of a man. No words. No Bio. No instructions. No choices. No 3-line Help Menu. Just a PHOTO of a man! What was I supposed to do next? This was strange. Do I touch the screen? Will a menu pop up if I do? I tapped with my finger. Nothing. I tapped a little harder. Oh! The photo jiggled. What?? That's odd. Now I have no instructions, no menu options, and I have a jiggly photo. Hmm. So I touched the photo again and must have moved my finger. The photo moved with my finger! (If you have used Tinder, I imagine you are either laughing right now or rolling your eyes – or both.) Then, something bizarre happened. I moved my finger, obviously a little too far to the right. All of a sudden, a burst came across the screen announcing something like, *Congratulations! You have a match!* And now allegedly I can communicate with said man behind the jiggly photo. WHAT?! How do you know I am a match with the person in the photo when I haven't reviewed his profile, I haven't given any permission for the man to contact me, and simply... what?! What is going on?

> What is the meaning, exactly, of the swipe? Swipe right means to like or accept someone, while swipe left means to reject them. The meaning of these two phrases is basically Tinder's core mechanics. If both people swipe right on each other, they'll be matched up.

Obviously, I did not know I should have completed research on Tinder's core mechanics prior to looking into their app! And I probably do not need to explain what happened next. At that moment I was able to see the man's profile and he was able to see mine. Now, I'm a writer, so of course I sounded completely awesome in my bio. Of course the man was interested in me. And of course that man was excited to see that I was, *yikes*, interested in him, too! Oh dear.

> ONLINE LESSON #1.
> LEARN DATE SITE MECHANICS FIRST

> ONLINE LESSON #2. HONESTY

Although I hated to burst the poor guy's bubble, it was the right thing to do. I politely let him know I was new and accidentally swiped right. At that point I had not yet learned you can remove profiles from your matched list. (See Lesson #1.)

> ONLINE LESSON #3. BE KIND

Regardless of the situation, I didn't want to be rude so I chatted with him briefly. He was nice, just truly not my type. My personal thoughts on chatting are that it is kind to give a brief reply to those who message you. It's okay to say thank you and let them know you're pursuing other matches. I've also heard it's not necessary to respond to messages you receive. I'm not sure what is appropriate, therefore, I always followed my personal nature *with boundaries*.

ONLINE LESSON #4. PROACTIVELY CREATE YOUR ESCAPE PLAN

Yikes. At this point I had not yet learned how to end things if someone overly engaged in the chatting. On the fly, I came up with the reason that *a friend had recommended I check out the site, but I wasn't quite ready.* And I wished him well… Oops, scratch Lesson #2 (Honesty) if you haven't prepped Lesson #4 (Exit Strategy), and you feel it's best to implement Lesson #3 (Kindness).

ONLINE LESSON #5. SAFETY

I don't recall feeling unsafe with the men I have met from online apps. However, I know my safety practices definitely improved over time. I'm a rather trusting person and I did have one scary moment when I was very new to dating. Not from online, but a lesson learned nonetheless which definitely applies here! In the situation, nothing happened and I was fine, but I did once have to physically push someone away who had completely misunderstood my friendliness one night. I later told one of my male co-workers what happened and he taught me a lesson with his response – *and* the fear in his face. I'll never forget him telling me severely, "You have to be careful!! These guys are *not* like the guys you know from church!"

I know times are different and you are likely a lot more aware than I was back then. However, please Google *Safety in Online Dating* and learn from the experts!

ONLINE LESSON #6:
SET YOURSELF UP FOR SUCCESS!

If you've heard wild stories about meeting people from dating apps, well, those stories are likely true! I have quite a few of my own I'll share with you. And before you start wondering WHY then do people even use this source?! There are many reasons. I can verify there are genuinely good people using online resources. I also know several happily married couples who've met online. Wild stories? Yes. Completely a lost cause? No, not at all. Many of us simply have types of careers or social networks that make it difficult to meet someone in our every day life and this avenue offers options. This method of meeting people also offers an opportunity for you to venture into dating at your own pace!

By implementing a few tips, you can easily minimize the bloopers and have a very successful experience. Here are some things I learned along the way...

Start by matching with someone who holds your same core values! This step alone will decrease your blooper experiences by 60%. – Okay, that is not truly a *proven* statistic; however, I think a research team would find it to be a fairly accurate percentage rate. If core values are not evident in someone's profile, pay attention to your conversation early on. If you bristle at something, ask questions!

I've noticed the initial interactions tell a lot about a person. Do they communicate well? Have a sense of humor? Too pushy? Slow to respond? Do they lack depth? Are they looking for a quick date or a potential relationship? Does the conversation flow or is it strained? If you don't seem to click with them comfortably, move on!

After a bit of interacting, you decide when you feel comfortable enough to give your cell number. An upstanding man will offer his first to help you feel more comfortable, and that phone call will be an important step before agreeing to meet in person. It is *completely* different to hear a voice and have conversation! Phone calls can be a make-or-break in your decision to take things further. You might get to this point and learn you are not such a match after all.

My guess is there are many people who have good phone conversations and next agree to meet in person. I've learned, however (after several failed meeting attempts), a video chat is a beneficial layer to add in the getting-to-know-you stage. See upcoming Bloopers section. *Oh my*, there are profile pictures, and then there is real life. Something like WhatsApp is both iPhone/Android compatible, and that video chat will prepare you far more realistically for your in-person meeting. Unless you like surprises. In that case, stick with your phone calls and enjoy the surprise! I mean, in all sincerity that can be fun. Then you'll have stories to share like the rest of us!

Kidding aside, I have one last note of lessons learned regarding your conversations. *Ask good questions!* This provides a greater compatibility check, thus reducing your blooper meter several more percentage points! Clarifying questions also give you opportunity to observe inconsistency in someone's portrayal of themselves. Above all, if you have red flags, there is probably a reason.

> I live at the beach and a Red Flag means
> *stay out of the water!*

Options

Hopefully, my ideas and tips are helping you feel more comfortable about the possibility of online dating. There are absolutely wonderful, honest men and women out there looking for companionship and partnership. That said, I do understand online dating may still seem like a less desirable way for you to meet someone.

If you're still unsure about online dating, let's look at the options:

- If you go to church, yes, a new single person could walk through those doors any Sunday. Outside of that, you already know the rest of the eligible singles.

- You could meet someone at the grocery store or Barnes & Noble... which could be as risky as the internet!

- If you are beyond college age, you are likely past the age where friends introduce mutual friends.

- At work? Please do not get me started on workplace romances. Remember my former career? It's not generally a good idea to pursue those options. (Check policies and proceed with caution!)

- Your community: Local sports clubs or singles meet-up groups. A larger church with a mid-life singles bible study. Maybe someone at the fitness center or pet park? If you are completely against going online, research your city for in-person opportunities. It may require taking up a new hobby or going outside your comfort zone, but opportunities to meet other singles are certainly out there.

I'm not here to promote one method or the other. What I would like you to know, though, is that singles are increasingly leveraging online dating as a more convenient alternative to meeting someone in person. It truly does not have the stigma it once had. If it's been a long time since you have gone on a date, this may be an opportunity to test the waters and get your sea legs. Whatever your age, if you have hesitation about dating sites, you can relax and give it a try. Almost 400 million others across the globe are giving it a try, too! If you don't know where to start, research a list of the different singles sites to view the focus of each community. You can simply search "compare different dating apps" and select one of the options to view the various perspectives. Once you find a site that feels like you, follow the steps to create a profile. Many apps have free options, so take advantage of that while you're learning. Be sincere, place a nice yet realistic photo of yourself, and just be you! Another option is to chat with your friends to see what apps they have used. You are likely to get some firsthand opinions... and a few fun stories, as well!

Bloopers

Speaking of stories... Should you decide to venture into, *or back into*, the virtual dating waters, leverage your good judgment and be prepared to enter relationships with realistic eyes before you decide to fall head over heels! While I truly have met some very nice men, I have had my fair share of *bloopers* shall we say. Here are some that have made my 5-star list, in no certain order.

It was always my preference to find a Christian man to match my personal beliefs. I was okay with different backgrounds but definitely wanted to find someone with similar core values to mine. Needless to say, that was a topic I would clarify fairly specifically before agreeing to meet in person.

One particular match had listed "Christian" on his profile and we had similar interests. We eventually talked on the phone, had good banter, a mutual respect related to our careers, and easy conversation. He was a local business owner in our city. Legitimate. (I checked before I accepted his lunch invitation.) Hmm, now where do I begin the list of *what went wrong* with this one?!

The mishaps started that day before the lunch date even began! The location was in a new area for me and, although using my GPS app, I missed a step just before the last turn to the restaurant. I texted him as soon as it happened. When I arrived, I discovered he was literally annoyed at me because I'd missed my turn, which caused me to show up 3 minutes late. Three minutes! Did I mention three *accidental* minutes? I thought he was kidding. Nope. He was not.

As I was trying to sort out what just happened, and attempting to make small talk, I mentioned how nice the restaurant was and that I had never eaten there before. *Ohh, the things you learn about someone while making small talk!* He continued to tell me how much he liked the restaurant, too, and that he ate there several times a week. I thought that sounded a little odd, so I responded.

Me: "Wow, you do?!"

Him: "Yes, this is where I have all my lunch dates."

Me: "All your lunch dates?"

Him: "Yes, I've had lunch with over 200 women from that site."

Me (perplexed): "Why??"

Him: "I just like having lunch with someone every day."

(Ahh, so this is 'lunch'. Not a lunch 'date'. Got it. Point taken.)

Me: "Oh. Wow."

I mean, *how* do you respond to your lunch date providing that kind of information?! I have more dating stories for you, and I'm not even finished with this guy yet! At one point, lunch had been ordered and, hindsight, I wish I would have left a 20 on the table and walked away. I think I didn't leave because it was so awkward, and I had not yet mastered Rule #4 (Create Your Escape Plan). Alas, I stayed and tried to find some redeeming quality to the meeting.

In my attempt to continue conversation, the topic of God came up, very lightly, more in comment. At the moment God was mentioned, I saw a peculiar look come across his face which made me take note. Having a carefree sense of humor, I laughed and said, "You *do* believe in God, don't you?" I was genuinely joking. I honestly can't remember what exactly came next, except that it led to some argumentative discussion about whether or not God was real. I was dumbfounded. Every time I tried to put the uncomfortable conversation to rest, he simply kept going. I then asked him why he labeled himself as "Christian" in his profile. – And that was the moment I learned some people hold a completely different definition from mine and Webster's. He equated the Christian label to mean he was, in general, a good person. Hmmm. Okay then.

As I was thinking back on this whole encounter, I remembered yet one more detail. At one point in the hour together, this allegedly "good person" somehow managed to work in that my body shape was not exactly what he was expecting. Yes, he really did that. Mind you, I am average and, at the time, I was happily a size 8. I'm okay with my size and understand some men like tiny women. I'm simply not tiny, so I make it extremely clear on my profile that I am average. I think I had even stated it so boldly as to say, *If you're looking for a Barbie doll, simply delete and move forward in your search.* (And for Pete's sake, please don't have the audacity to point it out to me in person!)

My Best Efforts

Needless to say, that experience taught me to ask questions with much more clarity in the future. Even then, when I thought I had clarified the important questions, still there were those who simply embellished their answers to please me. I'm not sure why. Maybe they so wanted to find someone that they rationalized it was okay to twist their answers in hopes I would change my mind once I met them in person. What they did not realize is, I won't change my mind, especially when we're talking about my beliefs and values – not to mention adding the poor character trait of *dishonesty* to your value system! Hard pass.

In spite of making my best efforts to clarify my values and preferences, mishaps continued. There was yet another Christian I had agreed to meet; this one even came in from out of town. I'm not a fan of long distance dating, and I think this was the turning point where I completely said *never again* outside the city limits! However, this particular gentleman had built enough connection with me, so I agreed to meet him. And then, during our dinner, I learned that he "*didn't really believe in God.*" What? But you listen to Andy Stanley! I am so confused.

And that wasn't the only thing that confused me that evening. I was also perplexed how this man had shrunk six inches from the time he left his hometown to the time he arrived into my city. Another preference I make incredibly clear is that I like to have a man taller than me. I feel very tall, although I'm not. Nonetheless, my profile, my life, my preferences. Now, if someone is 5'11" and I prefer 6' or over, that's okay! I simply want them to tell me truthfully they are 5'11" and, if we have chemistry, I will gladly meet them! What is not acceptable though, is to claim a height of 5'11" and in person show up at 5'5". Did that nice man (and he was genuinely very nice), did he think I would not notice the height discrepancy??

On another occasion, I was meeting someone local for dinner who had reached the restaurant quite a bit before I did. He was kind to call a few minutes early, letting me know he had gotten a table for us. That was great! When I arrived, I saw him at the table, he waved, and I smiled as I approached. He was just as handsome in person. The two of us had a wonderful dinner together. My career had some similarities to his so we meshed on several levels. Then the dinner ended and we stood up to leave. I had failed to realize that he had not gotten up to greet me when I arrived. We were so comfortable with each other, I hadn't thought anything about it.

And then we stood up to leave. I have no words at this point. This compatible, successful, man, was so short. I believe I was looking down at him! Again, it is one thing for me to have a preference. It is quite *another* thing to tell me something that is simply not true. I am about 5'5" on a good day, so if you say you are 5'10", I should not be looking down at you. My heels are not that high! At this point it is not about the height, it's about honesty. Where do you go with that? How do you build a relationship on that? I simply couldn't.

Another one of my 5-star bloopers... I was having dinner with a gentleman who looked somewhat older than I expected. I gave him the benefit of the doubt. I am aware that I have unique genes and look much younger. So maybe his genes are such that he looks much older. I'm aware we all simply age differently and that's okay. However, in the middle of our date, the man himself mentioned his age to me – which was 8 years older than his profile! I'm not opposed to a man being a few years older, but those few years are my limit on age gap. It was a slightly bewildering moment learning someone would be that dishonest about their age, so I quite boldly expressed my frustration.

His response? He claimed it was to attract females in the age range he prefers. He said if he put his actual age, only older women would match up with him. *Yes, you read that right.* He actually said that. Then he proceeded to tell me that he always explains that to the women when he talks with them and he had "explained all that before we met." Umm, no. No mister. There was no explanation. Because if there had been an explanation, I would not be sitting here.

Enjoy the Experience

I'm confident I have enough stories to fill another book; however, I'm sure you are capturing that, in spite of our best efforts, *bloopers happen!* If you are safe, that is really the most important thing. Inevitably, you will end up with some funny stories of your own. I know my hairstylist used to love my visits. I'll never forget her laughing at one of my stories saying, "Michelle, you never disappoint!"

Sure, things will occasionally happen or take a twist when you least expect it. At times, you might discover the compatibility you want is simply not there. Other times, you may simply discover a wonderful friend. It's best to enjoy the companionship while keeping realistic expectations. Then one day, you truly may meet the one who is your match. And remember, they will have ventured out taking that first awkward step just like you!

NEXT STEPS

Something to think about...

What are your thoughts about online dating? Scary, not your style, fun, entertaining? What if your future partner is out there having the same thoughts?

Something to move forward...

If online dating feels uncomfortable, what local avenues might you venture into? Either way you decide to venture, which tips can help you minimize potential bloopers with a new date introduction?

Something to do...

Whether you venture online or stick with traditional meetings, it's a good idea to be prepared for the unexpected if a date turns into a 5-star Blooper. Create your Escape Plan!

Kidding aside, there truly are genuine people using this avenue.
Be smart and have fun!

11

The 20-Mile Radius

"There is NO ONE worth dating in this town!"

Does that sound familiar? If there is one consistent dating complaint I've heard through the years, it has to be this one! People say they would enjoy finding a good quality person to date and there appears to be virtually no one in their community. Well, guess what? I'm not here to suggest you need to look harder or lower your standards. I agree, there are some communities which truly do not seem to have any significant number of quality single people.

It could also be your community simply does not have anyone with similar interests to you. I once met a business man who lived in a suburb of a larger city. He tried online dating and ran into this same issue. He said all the females in his area liked to hunt, fish, and wash their corvettes. Mind you, there is nothing wrong with hunting, fishing, *or corvettes*; it just wasn't his style for finding a partner with mutual hobbies and a compatible relationship. He knew he had to widen his search... and that's how he met me!

Unfortunately, this is truly a dilemma. If you are finding yourself ready to enjoy partnership again, it's frustrating to have no one of interest in your area. I hear this so frequently. There seems to be a true lack of good solid singles in social circles, as well as local online searches. If it's not the lack in quality of a person, it's a problem finding compatibility to your core values, interests, or life stage. This predicament is both disappointing and sad. And where does it leave you? Sitting home alone, bored on Saturday nights, and going through life without partnership to share your days.

If you have found yourself in this situation, there are a few options to consider. **Option 1**, of course, is to merely accept being alone and focus on living a rewarding life solo. Rather than partnership, you can learn to enjoy strong local *friendships*. There are advantages to being single and you might discover you enjoy it!

Are there other options? Well, yes. **Option 2**: You could wait it out and hope a special someone moves to town. Bear in mind that might not happen on your time table, though. And that leads us to **Option 3**: Thinking outside the box, or rather, outside your community. By the way, if this option doesn't sound like you, stick with me for a few minutes. There's more to this radius chapter than meets the eye! (We'll call it **Option "3b"**.)

After the last chapter, I fully understand, you may not want to hear the details of Option "3a". However, I like to be both encouraging *and* realistic. So here is my realistic encouragement: The first step to thinking outside of your community begins with venturing into your dating app. As awkward or frustrated as you might feel about this, it's time to venture. Realistically, if you have no one in your town (and you truly want to find a partner), it's time to step outside your comfort zone. If you haven't done this yet, find a dating app that fits your lifestyle, and create yourself an online profile! Once completed, your next stop will be in the settings feature.

> Go to your profile settings and widen your radius!
> (That is not a figure of speech, by the way.)

Right now you're frustrated over the fact that there are no quality eligible singles in your 20-mile radius. Every time you look around in your community, you get the same results. There is no one! Time passes. You look again. Still no one. A few months later you try again. None. Do you really want to keep repeating this??

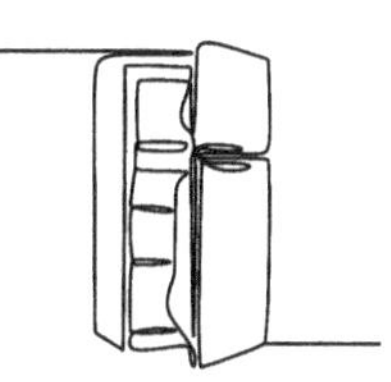

That is the same scenario as those times you repeatedly go to your refrigerator hoping a terrific snack will appear. You know what I'm talking about. I've done it. I will repeatedly open the frig door expecting one of those times to find just what I'm craving. However, if the food is not in there the first time, the food is not going to be in there. It doesn't matter how many times I open that door. After a bit, I have to accept it.

And there you have it. Your choices are to either go hungry or hop in the car and head for the grocery store! It's your decision.

Obviously, a trip to the grocery store is much simpler than considering a relationship in a neighboring city. The concept, though, is the same! If you've looked in all the right places and still there is no one compatible, chances are, each time you look there will likely still be no one compatible. If that's consistently been the case, and you are serious about finding partnership, it may take venturing into...

Option #3a: Widening your radius. I mean that literally, by the way. The radius in your dating app. You probably know that your settings can be adjusted to search for singles in your general 20-mile radius. *The geographical area where you are saying there is no one to be found.* If that's where you have your current settings, it may be time to increase your range to add in a larger city and thus, a larger pool of eligible singles. Note, I don't recommend a nationwide search unless you are open to moving across the country (and you have a lot more faith than I do). Most likely, though, you will see a difference if you merely increase enough to pull in the next larger city away from you. – More opportunity. Definitely realistic!

> **Option #3b**: As promised. If you think this topic of "Long Distance" does not pertain to you and you've sworn off dating apps, that's okay, too. Please keep hanging with me here! I've personally known more than a few people who have reunited with friends or love interests from their past who were *not* on a dating app. Oh, I just remembered, that even happened to me once! We live in a world where people relocate and later find themselves reconnecting with those from a former season of life. In today's world of communication, it may be best to read on and be prepared!

By the way, if a connection happens outside of your 20-mile radius, regardless of how it happens, the relationship *can* be successful. It just takes a little smart planning and realistic expectations. I was surprised to learn that long distance relationships are similar to traditional relationships with an average 60% success rate! I, on the other hand, did not personally have this success rate... but then again, neither did I have smart planning *or* realistic expectations!

Tough Questions

I'm not sure I had ever proactively planned to meet someone outside of my local area. I rather *stumbled into it* through my inexperience on the dating app, and it was initially fun and entertaining. The good news is that some of those fun experiences did develop into friendships. As I began to enjoy those friendships on a deeper level, though, it led me to consider the possibility of actual long distance dating.

While I was very much in the right place emotionally, I was not truly in the right place logically. The friendships had started off playful so initially the distance didn't matter. I had not considered, "What if my heart gets involved and now there are feelings, along with distance and careers and homes and families?" I should have taken a step back to process where I was headed. But alas, *hindsight.*

I encourage you to walk yourself through the below reflection questions. Even if you would not consider long distance dating *online*, I can't stress enough about the possibility of someone reaching out from your past. It can happen out of the blue and, before you know it, you may be looking at possibilities! Even if you think you could never get seriously attached to someone long distance, think again. If anything, the emotional connections can be more meaningful. Your focused conversations are not interrupted by the in-person distractions of everyday life. This often allows long distance communication to run deeper and more meaningful.

These reflection questions will keep you grounded emotionally, hopefully adding a layer of protection around your heart. It warrants taking a pause before your possibilities begin...

Question: *Are you in a life space where you can realistically see yourself relocating?*

Visualize what that would look like. Resigning or transferring from your current job. Moving away from neighbors you enjoy and trust. Moving from your kids or grandkids. You will miss future special events or spend quite a bit financially traveling back for them. Transferring to new doctors and hospital systems. Moving your pets. And, although this one sounds trivial, changing the stores where you currently shop or losing your favorite restaurant! Adjusting to new traffic patterns and new streets. Possibly adjusting to a new climate!

These are a few of the daily life areas to consider. It's neither good nor bad, merely a step in visualizing life relocated to a new city.

If you are open and ready for a new start like this, it can be a fun and meaningful dating adventure! It will also be a bit of a process, so be sure to visualize that, too. The more you can visualize, the more realistic and successful you can be. If there is a great distance, this can mean overnight stays and travel expense, as well. Before you let your heart get too far down the road (pardon the pun), think through how you will create your in-person visits to minimize the burden falling too heavily on either one of you.

Q: *Do you think you could possibly develop a long distance relationship if the other person is willing to relocate to your area?*

Long distance doesn't mean *you* have to be the one relocating. If staying put is a non-negotiable for you, it's still okay for you to pursue a long distance relationship! Just be sure this topic comes up early in conversations with a new potential partner to ensure you are both on the same page. Then, be considerate. If it works out, and they are willing to relocate for you, remember they will be the one now adjusting to all of the items we just mentioned.

Q: *Can you feel satisfied with long stretches between affection?*

You will likely develop a strong emotional bond when you meet someone who lives a distance away. Without the distraction of "doing" things in person, your relationship will be greatly built on communication and caring for each other. That said, you will also miss a degree of physical affection. Longer stretches between kisses and having arms around you. Nights alone curling up under the blanket on your sofa. If physical touch is important to you, this is an aspect of long distance to consider. You may have no partner at events when schedules don't coordinate. In essence, while you *have* someone, you have them a lesser amount of physical time. On the positive side, though, if the relationship works out, this will only be a phase. You will later have the benefit of your strong emotional base.

Q: *Will you trust someone and feel secure during your times apart?*

Each of you will have your individual lives happening while you're apart. Job. Friends. Events. Yard work. Shopping. Family. Appointments. Etc. There will be times when you call or text and they won't respond right away. You may think you know their schedule but, as you know, sometimes things come up or phone calls go long and it's not easy to respond quickly. If communication and trust are a big deal for you, this could be a challenge. On the other hand, if you have a confident, trusting personality, and realistic expectations, you will probably not even notice a lull in response time.

Q: *Can you get to know a man out of his everyday environment?*

You will most likely develop a rich, meaningful emotional connection with your long distance partner. What you miss, however, is seeing them in their everyday setting. Even if your relationship is with someone from your past, they may have changed over the years. When we're not around someone every day, we may not realize how their routines or habits might clash with ours. It could be as simple as not folding the towel neatly after drying their hands. If you are rather tidy, little habits like this can become annoying. They may jump up and rinse dishes right after eating, where you prefer to sit and chat after meals. With your limited physical interaction, these are the patterns which will take more learning and adjusting from both of you when you're together. Do not underestimate the impact of quirks and habits!

After evaluating some of these nuances of long distance dating, you can determine if you think this might be an option for you. If it is not, *keep your radius set to 20 miles!* It is much better to stay put and develop a rewarding life with yourself, friends, and family. If you do decide to venture out, be honest, be smart, and be realistic. Long distance relationships can be truly rewarding!

Things Will Happen

With all the pre-planning in the world, though, there are still going to come into your long distance situations things you could not have prepared for. I've seen this myself and with friends. Some good. Some sad. Some that make your eyes roll. And others that are simply mouth dropping. I couldn't very well create this chapter without sharing a few of them...

On an eye-rolling note, there was the man I had been talking with for several months who lived a couple hours away from me. His location was realistic, we were both business minded, had similar core values, and we communicated very well together. The potential for a relationship was definitely there. We had also exchanged several photos with each other, so no surprise there either. Or was there? The time finally came when we could coordinate a visit. I was going to be in his city on business; a great way to meet each other without either one having to make a long drive.

With all we had in our favor, and all the conversations, you might think this visit would have been the first of many! Unfortunately, our first visit was also the last. The reason? – I wasn't blonde.

He informed me he was used to dating blondes. Yes. You read that all correctly... especially the line where I said we had exchanged several photos. – I have nothing else to say.

You've heard the expression... *"You can't make that up!"*

You, too, will have some of these experiences, and I promise there is good in between. When the bizarre events happen, you simply have to laugh, accept it, share it with a friend, and move on.

I had a guy friend who developed a long distance relationship with a woman out-of-state from where he lived. At one point, he was invited to a friend's wedding which happened to be located in a town not far from the girlfriend. Not only was this a great way for them to finally meet, they also made plans to go to his friend's wedding together. When the weekend arrived, he flew to Maryland. Upon arrival, he called the woman to let her know he'd landed. She then informed him she had injured her leg and would not be able to go to the wedding with him. Of course he was disappointed, but he certainly understood. He then proceeded to drive to her house to meet her and check in on her. Upon arriving, the woman's *sisters* came to the door! She had her sisters interact with him and refused to come out to meet him. Needless to say, he attended the wedding Minus One and flew back home, minus one, also.

And Then, *Things Will Happen*

Be prepared! There will be times when you *do* have a great meeting experience. At one point, when online dating was new to me, I decided to have my go with a site. I'm not sure I was specifically looking for either local or long distance. (I probably should have considered that in advance!) I merely completed the profile sections, checking the boxes where it asked which qualities I was looking for in a partner. Once I'd finished, it didn't take long before my profile was somehow matched with Mike's. *Ahh*, Mike. We had similar backgrounds, the same core values, several things in common, and we even worked in the same career field.

It started with a greeting. Then there were chats. Then phone calls. Our communication was meaningful and easy, and we were undeniably compatible. The catch? He lived several states away from me and I had kids in college. 'Not the end of the world, but definitely something to consider.

Nonetheless, he captured my heart and I was willing to figure it out. It wasn't long before he was able to reroute one of his business trips so we could meet in person. As expected, we blended effortlessly and the attraction to each other was mutual. As soon as possible, he scheduled another rerouting so we could see each other again.

Our conversations continued, as did the plan for continued visits. There was no doubt this was the type of partner I had been looking for. We merely had to figure out how to make the distance work, and I had to decide if I really could move away from my kids. Even though they were grown, they were still young and I absolutely loved spending time with them. But my heart. My heart was captured by this man, and it had been for several months.

Then, about 8 months into our relationship, something shifted. I don't remember exactly what it was, but I knew it was different. One day soon after, with every bit of genuine apology, he updated me on what had happened. Without trying, he met someone quite unexpectedly in his home town. It was not what he planned, but he did admit it was better for him to have someone there in person. I cannot begin to explain how absolutely crushed I was. I truly thought God had brought this person into my life. In spite of the long distance between us (albeit that was a hurdle), we were a complete match. I was heartbroken. What made it worse, there was no change about feelings; it was merely that he was at a place in life where he needed an in-person relationship and someone stepped in who could fill the gap.

That was my first full experience of dating someone long distance. If you think it's not possible to have a relationship, feelings, and a genuine love for someone across the miles, I can verify, long distance relationships are real. When he and I had met in person, our chemistry together confirmed the compatibility and connection we had already discovered over the phone. Little did I realize then, a breakup from a long distance relationship can hurt *every bit* as much as a local relationship.

As with any breakup, I pulled myself up by the bootstraps and took time to heal. I removed myself from the dating site and really didn't date much for a while. After some time had passed, however, I began to wonder if Mike had continued his new relationship. I wondered if maybe it didn't work out and he simply didn't tell me. After all, he did explain the long distance was challenging for him so of course he likely wouldn't communicate. Still, I was curious. And what do you do when you're young and curious? You go back to the dating site, create yourself a new profile, and look to see if that person is back there on the dating scene! And so I did.

Within minutes of my profile being back on the site, one of the single men sent me a very nice note. Oh dear, I wasn't expecting that! However, Online Lesson #2 kicked in, HONESTY. I thanked the nice man for his note and let him know I wasn't really *looking* for anyone, but rather I was snooping to see if a past boyfriend had put his profile back on the site. He laughed, thanked me for my honesty, and somehow we picked up a conversation together.

It's funny how life can take a turn when you least expect it. Or should I say, it's funny how God can step in and give you someone special when life's bumps have hit you the hardest. There I was still slightly hurt and frustrated. I was not looking for a new date or even a new friend, yet there appeared this person. I have no idea what we chatted about. Ha, probably the craziness of long distance dating! Nonetheless, we chatted, and then we chatted more. He helped me with guy advice, and I helped him with girl advice. Over time and more chats we exchanged numbers and had calls together. At the time, I was more of a firecracker and he was rather laid back compared to me. Although we had things in common, core values, and similar level of intellect, I think our personality differences kept us in the wonderful place of genuine friendship with each other. Generally, long distance relationships are romantic. This one, however, was a wonderful surprise and I gained the dearest friend. We were literally friends for seven years before we ever met in person!

Through the years we have remained good friends. Did we have moments when the friendship crossed over to possibly more? Did we spend some of that time in person? Yes, we did. Our personalities over time meshed closer together and we had mutual attraction. For different reasons, though, we have remained as friends. Sometimes you accept that timing and distance are not always on your side. We each dated other people through the years. We have both given to each other endless advice about our dating choices, and we've had each other's care and support when things went bad. Although there were glimpses of taking our friendship to another level, you have to be mature and accept that, as it is with your friendships across town, sometimes friendships across the distance are also not meant to be more. To this day, we are still friends from our funny beginning on the match site, and I wouldn't trade a day of it.

What's Right for You

In the end, you will decide what's right for you. You may want to try the long distance adventure. If that's the case and you're ready, go widen that dial on your radius! If you are unable to relocate or don't care to walk this path, keep your eyes open. There may be someone just around the corner.

Or you may be at the place in life where you accept the reality that you truly may not find anyone in your smaller town. Your decision may be to focus on the blessings of your current life and making the most of every day solo. The single again life can actually be a rewarding time of self-reflection and renewal.

I had to go through a spell of re-evaluation myself. After a few long distance experiences, both online *and* with someone from my past, I reached a point where I decided long distance was not for me. I lived in a small town, so I knew what this decision meant. It was time to accept my life would most likely be alone. It was not how I pictured my life to turn out, yet I had to accept reality. And my reality was I had a lot of blessings for which to be grateful! Above all, I had the best family anyone could ask for. And I had so much more. I'd recently been able to buy my fixer upper near the beach, a goal I had planned for 15 years. I had a terrific church, wonderful neighbors, and I'd lived an amazing career. My life was full in so many other ways. I simply had reached a place in life where it was not reasonable to consider moving. I knew the outcome could mean living the rest of life alone. I came to peace with that, dialed my radius back to 20 miles, and eventually turned off the dating app altogether.

The choice is yours. If you can't relocate or don't want to risk your heart, please choose life solo with your chin up and look upon all the blessings in life that your 20-mile radius has to offer!

NEXT STEPS

Something to think about...

Do you think you have truly exhausted all the resources for meeting someone in your local area? Would you consider dating someone long distance?

Something to move forward...

Sometimes we have to stay put in our current town, and the dating choices may be slim. What things can you be grateful for in your life while you're waiting for Prince Charming to arrive?

Something to do...

Take yourself through the "Tough Questions" at the beginning of this chapter and physically write out your answers. What conclusion do you reach about your local dating pool??

What are you going to do with your 20-mile radius??

12

Emotions With Kids

My fingers are tapping on the keys of the keyboard. Not typing. Just tapping. Mmm. Tap tap tap. Bits of thoughts zipping through my mind. Reminders of the past. Emotions I've experienced. Conversations I've had. Decisions I've witnessed. Things I want to share. Stories. Opinions. From kids. From parents. From partners. Hurts. Sweetness. Frustration. Successes. Bitterness. Love. Walls. Sadness. Such a sensitive area of our lives and one that touches almost all of us at every stage. – *Kids.*

What a range of emotions. I have witnessed these emotions and have had many conversations about kids throughout my single years. The interesting thing, though? *Not once* were they limited to a range of age!

When it comes to kids, so many experiences in our everyday world are labeled with age limits. Toys recommended for ages 3+... Kids Menu 12 and under... Bounce Houses safe for 3 to 12-year-olds... Theme Park tickets free for ages 2 and under... But when it comes to divorce, loss of a parent, and parents starting over??

> There is *no age limit* to the impact on kids.

"I cried last week because you weren't here and I thought you wasn't comin' back." –*Young daughter*

"You were like the only mom he ever had." –*A grown daughter*

"My kids are angry because they think I moved on too soon." –*Widower*

"Whew, those kids were not happy he remarried and now she'll get their inheritance." –*Friend of the gossips*

"I've not told the kids we're dating. They've been through enough." –*Boyfriend*

"I don't want to date until my daughter is out of high school." –*Divorced man*

"In your book, tell the parents to not talk bad about the other parent in front of their children. Keep your bitterness to yourself. That is not for a child to bear." –*Grown daughter of divorced parents*

"My ex talks mean about me; then the kids and grandkids come over and talk mean the same way." –*Divorced woman*

"The ex-wife will use the children. When you remarry, you marry *the family!*" –*New wife*

"No, I don't want to go to dinner. I don't want to meet him." –*Granddaughter*

Kids of every age and stage in life have feelings and opinions about their parent, their parent's choices, and especially their parent's relationships. Those parents, in turn, also form opinions and make decisions based on how they think their kids might be feeling. However, the feelings between the two don't always match up!

There are parents who think their kids are not ready for a new parent figure, yet they are. Other parents move on without consideration and the kids get thrown into an emotional roller coaster. You've heard the phrase, *kids are resilient.* The reality is, kids are not always resilient, and this saying does not apply to only younger children. In my relationships that were a bit more difficult to navigate, the kids were grown. One older teen came right out and told me she wouldn't get close to me because she learned that, "you get close to someone and then they leave." She was right. Three years later, I did.

Kids, loss, and relationships. What a sensitive topic. Children adapting to new relationships has its complexities and they are tangled for sure! When kids lose a special parent figure in life, it can pull at their heart and impact them in more ways and for longer time than most of us realize. At all ages, kids hurt. Kids love. They get angry. Kids get tangled in our messes. They experience deep and lasting emotions. At all ages, parents make choices impacting those kids. And amid these packed emotions, we face the juggle of our decisions in moving forward with life.

Kids and Communication

As I was initially thinking about the topics for this book, I knew I wanted to include a chapter on *Kids*. Even though mine were teens when I got divorced, I dated men with younger children and the experiences had a significant impact on my life. I learned there is a lot of love out there with our kids, and there is also a lot of hurt. I learned that kids at every age have opinions and emotions when their parents start dating. ...I also learned that appropriate and meaningful conversations can minimize many of those escalated emotions – from 3 to 63. Regardless of age, never underestimate the power of a gentle conversation.

Note, it's not that kids need to have a *say* in our decisions; rather, it's that a level of respect and communication with them can make all the difference in lessening the *impact* of our decisions. When we have conversations up front, it offers the opportunity for our families to express their emotions and address any surprising feelings that may surface.

And by the way, not all of of your conversations will be negative! I remember telling my son I felt guilty about dating. He responded that he liked it when I went out, because then *he* didn't feel guilty going out with his friends leaving me home alone! I never would have thought about his perspective had I not brought up the subject.

Not every conversation with your family may go as smoothly, however. If you anticipate a rocky conversation about moving forward or you are uncertain how to approach it, I encourage you to seek out a sounding board. This could be simply chatting ideas with a friend or with your hairstylist. Or, if you genuinely have escalated emotions in your family, consider talking it over with a professional counselor or life coach to help you navigate the conversation. When it comes to our kids, it's probably better to learn from guidance rather than from mistakes!

> It's not so much, should you or shouldn't you date, but rather it is *how* you go about moving forward that will make the difference in taming heightened emotions.

You Have a Heart, Too

While the emotions of your kids are greatly important, and they do warrant a level of your respect, please be aware of your own emotions and your loneliness. Your desires for partnership are *equally* important! As delicately as I can say this, your kids are priority... and YOU are, too.

You have gone through loss of a partner. You are facing life solo now and it can be extremely lonely. I know it is natural to put kids first when they are involved, especially if they have endured a divorce, death, or even a serious breakup. We want to protect our kids from more hurt. This is admirable, yes. It is also important to address and acknowledge your *own* hurts and desires.

I've known people who have completely put their personal lives on hold thinking they were protecting the experience of their children. While every situation is unique, when handled appropriately, it is possible to prioritize our kids' hearts while also tending to our own. You deserve love and partnership and, kids or not, you should feel free to move forward with dating when you're ready. Just remember the importance of proceeding with love, respect, and mature communication.

Younger Children... *Even Grandchildren*

[A special note: This section was written to address younger children. If you are closer to the age where you have or may be involved with grandchildren, I encourage you to read on through those eyes. The emotions are the same, if not more so.]

If your kids are younger, please be aware that your decision to move forward with dating may add a layer of emotions related to love, loyalty, and potentially an amount of confusion. As your new life settles in without your spouse around, your kids will be learning to love each of you in a new *individual* way. You can imagine adding the complexity, then, when one of you begins to date. This brings a whole new layer of feelings and emotions, especially for a younger child to experience – and not all of these emotions will be negative!

While some kids may react in hesitation, others will welcome and adore the new person. You can imagine the conflict of emotions then, when your child is placed in the situation of a new parent figure entering the family relationship. If your child enjoys them, they may feel guilty or they may interpret their own emotions as having a lack of loyalty toward the other parent. This is when healthy communication and open conversations will again be key in helping your kids process through their emotions.

Now let's consider what happens with the emotions when it is your ex-husband who begins to date. First of all, if you go through this experience, your *own* emotions will want to run wild. And probably not in the same direction as your children! This is normal. Even if you wanted the separation, even if it's been a long time, it is human for this experience to sting when you see your former spouse happy in a new relationship.

Then, let's add in the next layer. How will you respond seeing your *kids* happy in the new relationship? That goes beyond a sting! Your own emotions might run deep in anger, jealousy, hurt, or envy. If this happens, take a deep breath. Stop to consider your kids' feelings and ensure their emotions are being acknowledged (while separating your own). If you see your kids feeling conflicted, ask if they would like to talk about it. This conversation may be tough on you, yet it will be ever important for you to remain as neutral as possible.

To clarify... **Neutral.** *Unbiased. Impartial. Not taking sides.*

Note! This is not the time to dig the scoop from your children. It will be tempting, yes. But appropriate?? Remember, the focus is on helping your child adjust. This conversation is to help them feel comfortable and guilt-free about enjoying a new parent figure in their life. It's your moment to reassure them that it's okay and you know they still love *you* just as much.

As hard as it might be, if your kids love the new person, let them love them. Ultimately, that is a good thing! And what, then, do you do with your own emotions? Well, this would be an excellent time to go find your best friend – preferably when the kids are not within earshot!

Remember, one day you may be that new extra mom to someone else's children! I have been in more than one dating relationship where kids were involved. The kids adored me and that was important. It was nothing at all against their mom. It's that I was in a relationship where we spent time together, and I wanted the kids to feel comfortable. Not once did I ever detect they loved me more or thought any less of their own mom.

I have the sweetest of memories... Teaching one how to tie his shoes. Buying a daughter her first purse. Giving piggy back rides. Trips to McDonald's. Trips to the beach. Hiking in the woods looking for hidden treasure. Turning monkey bars into spaceships and landing on the moon. Watching T-ball games. Sitting on the porch swing late at night, listening to the crickets, and talking about life with a teenage son. Shopping for ornaments to decorate the tree for *us girls.* Snuggling with a story and tucking kids in at night. Watching a daughter's band come down the street in the Christmas parade. Baking brownies together. Holidays. Birthdays. Meals. Adventures. Hugs. Kisses. Sweet memories.

These are the experiences you create to help children feel comfortable and balanced in their somewhat unbalanced world.

May I add, when your ex begins to date, you should only hope that the new woman will do the same for your kids. Likewise, if you begin to date someone with children, I hope you will also create the the same special moments. From 2 to 32, the age does not matter. What matters is relationship. What matters is a young child feeling safe and loved. What matters is an older daughter knowing her father is with a good person who will not take advantage of him. Doing the right thing is always the right thing.

If you are one step ahead of me, you might be wondering, *What happens if the relationship doesn't work out?* Are these memories that you miss?? Yes. They are memories that I miss with every bit of my heart. At the same time, are they memories I would trade because some of those relationships didn't work out? No, I wouldn't trade them. I couldn't have known the future and, while I was in the relationships, it was right for me to ensure those kids had experiences and memories. I also felt blessed to have had the love of those kids.

What then do you do with all the love and memories if the relationship takes a turn and comes to an end? Well, there isn't any way to say this gently. You hurt for a time. One of the hardest parts for me was that I was not able to say goodbye to some of them. I was inexperienced so I hadn't thought through how I would process a breakup. *It would have been nice to have had the Instruction Manual, but I didn't.*

I think if there had been the manual back then, the Dating & Children section would have read something like this:

> As you enter a relationship where kids are involved, have a conversation with your partner up front and agree how you will communicate with the children should the relationship come to an end. Ensure that you will have the opportunity to say goodbye to the children. In the goodbye, lovingly communicate to the children involved that sometimes adults learn they are not always a good match for each other and they decide to stop dating. Reassure them how much you love them and focus on the memories you will always have with you. End on a happy note and big hugs.

If this seems too hard or inappropriate for you, maybe you can take these words and ask their father to please relay the message. Don't assume a man will know how to handle communicating the breakup. – He may appreciate the tip.

Unfortunately, I did not have the manual or the advice. Nor did I have the experience to proactively think through an agreement like this. Still, I would not trade any of the memories or exciting adventures. But if I'm being honest, does it hurt when there is loss? Yes. Very much. And so I pause as I type. To cry just a little. You know, you can have love and sadness at the same time. That's what I'm feeling right now.

Bitter-sweet. adjective: *a complex, mixed emotion of experiencing happiness and sadness, joy and sorrow, or pleasure and regret simultaneously. It often refers to nostalgic or poignant moments that are simultaneously heartwarming and painful.*

If They Only Knew

If you experience a break from a relationship where kids are involved (at any age), one of the most challenging aspects of this is that the kids will never truly understand all your heart has been through – and you will leave that information alone! If you ever find yourself caught between wishing kids understood the situation and yet wondering how much to tell them, even if you want to spill all those ugly beans about your ex, take another one of those deep breaths. Ask yourself, "Is this their fight? How might this impact them?" Then, take your bitterness and anger to an appropriate source for help – which is not the children. There are conversations you can and should have with kids, and hanging dirty laundry is not one of them.

This would be the time to consider the option of finding your best friend or a Life Coach. Telling children about the situation, regardless of how horrible your relationship was, is most likely going to be inappropriate. First, it is not for kids to bear. It is *your* situation! Secondly, it is not right to place that weight on a child (at any age). Think about it. If you do tell personal things about their father, what exactly are they supposed to do with the information? Offer you advice?? Choose to side with you? And then once they take on all the new emotion, where do they get to go to unload it?? There may be times you'll want kids to know *exactly* what their parent is like. I highly encourage you in those moments, however, to take a deep breath and consider the outcome for them. Lastly, even if you would try to give explanation, they still will not have walked in your shoes. Take the high road and find the appropriate outlet for your anger and hurt.

Hopefully, you've processed similar thoughts in regards to this topic and have made the decision to refrain from sharing information with any kids involved in your past relationships. That's a wise decision, even when their lack of knowledge might cause them to form an unfavorable opinion toward you and your decision about moving forward. If you are facing this frustration, truly the frustration is real! And yet it's still the better frustration to experience. Consider the alternative. If you discuss your relationship with kids, at any age or to any depth, your story will appear one-sided and you will inevitably come out the bad guy. If you must, talk it out privately with another trusted adult.

– *Breakups are a topic for a good girls night out!*

Moving Forward

Always the big question... *When is it appropriate* to move forward after a loss of relationship, especially when kids are involved? Is it different with younger children versus older kids? Is moving on from a breakup different from divorce? How different is that when the loss was through death??

I was a little surprised, yet glad to learn, that the old thoughts of waiting a lengthy period are now no longer advised! I still agree it is not wise to rush into a relationship; however, I have a healthy respect for each person's individual situation. What you will find is, a wait period of about 6 months is encouraged for younger kids to have time to adjust and feel safe in their new lifestyle. It is also suggested to not introduce every date to children, rather wait about 6 months to ensure it's going to likely be a stable relationship. Based on my personal experience, I like this advice.

As for widows, this can be a very personal decision and it is not one for others to judge. If you had a spouse who had an extensive illness or you are a younger parent left with children, you may move on faster than what others may deem comfortable. What I say to that is... they have not walked in your shoes!

> It's possibly been years since you have had a relaxing evening out or gone to an event with a partner.

If you are now a single parent, no one can comprehend the load you juggle. As long as you give your children time to grieve and adapt and you keep the communication open, you have the right to live your life. People who are going to judge, are going to judge. But this is your life, not theirs, and your heart deserves to have love, support, and companionship.

Regardless of how you have become single again, only you know your heart and your personal desires. Moving forward is your decision. (If you struggle with this, go back and re-read the first 4 chapters.) No one has walked in your exact shoes – including your children!

Is moving forward sometimes a juggling act when kids are involved, *at any age*? Yes, it is. Do we need to have some amount of balance and respect? Yes, we do. Within boundaries and good communication, though, it is your life to live. And I wish you all the happiness in finding new love and companionship.

NEXT STEPS

Something to think about...

How would you feel about getting involved with someone who is close to their children or grandchildren?

Something to move forward...

What kids in your world, old or young, might need a gentle, open conversation with you?

Something to do...

Think about the questions, concerns, and emotions your kids might be experiencing. With these in mind, plan some future conversations with each one.

Need to get it off your chest?
Best friends and life coaches – Great options!

13

Windshields Have the Better View!

If I could have tucked a pack of pixie dust on one specific page in this book, *this page* would definitely be the one! You are likely reading here because you have been thrown into a life category you had neither planned nor wanted: *Single Again*. You were in a relationship and now, for whatever the reason, you are not. You are alone and living life solo. Regardless of how you feel right at this moment about dating and starting over, at some point you will most likely find yourself desiring companionship and beginning a new relationship.

– *Enter Pixie Dust.*

On the night of your next first date, I would have you turn to this page, slip out the packet, dip your fingers, and delightfully sprinkle that goodness from the top of your head to the tips of your toes. I can see it now, sparkles swirling and engulfing your being. Blessing you with a solid, stable, fun, compatible, meaningful relationship.

Oh, if only I could have included that envelope in your purchase. As we know, though, relationships don't generally go overnight from first magical date to happily ever after. The prince does not typically seek you out the next day with your missing glass slipper and sweep you back to his castle.

No, in the real world, there is a date and then maybe there is another. And then, if there is potential, a new relationship begins to form with time and practice. Time spent together, time talking, learning, adjusting, and growing together. There will be the initial attraction and companionship in a new dating relationship. Then life settles in where patterns and boundaries begin to develop. You discover likes and dislikes. You try new things together. There's a blend of compromise and support. If these stages show strong compatibility, the relationship progresses, and true partnership begins.

There is in this process, however, the possibility of discovering some areas of your lives which are not as compatible. You may discover character traits that are not in alignment with your values. There may be conflict of long-term life goals. In time, unfortunately, it is a possibility the two of you may reach a decision to end the relationship.

I wish I didn't have to write these pages.

I do have to write them, though. While I dearly love my popcorn and a good Hallmark movie, real life dating relationships do not always hold those last ten minutes of your favorite rom-com. You know them. When the man realizes the misunderstanding, changes his mind, and goes running after the girl.

Sadly, not every real life beginning has an ending where the two end up together. And I want to help you navigate this experience when it happens to you. Because at that moment, you will then be single again, *again*.

> I have walked in those shoes. I have walked in those shoes until the soles wore thin.

Breaking Up is Hard to Do

In 1962, Neil Sedaka released the cutest song, "Breaking Up is Hard to Do." The words begin with those familiar doo-wops and bops we recognize from that era. If you're too young to remember, I'd love for you to pull this up on YouTube. The tune to this song is simply adorable. If you don't pay full attention to the lyrics, you'll be bobbing your head from the first few notes. If you do remember the song, have a break from reading here and take a jog down memory lane... I'll see you in two and a half minutes.

Welcome back. Was that song a rolled up mix of emotions? A mix of catchy tune with your shoulders swaying to the beat, yet listening to simply heartbreaking words? I'd venture to say it might have even caused you to tear up. Why they wrote this scenario to such a fun tune, I have no idea! The reality is, when you go through a breakup, it is anything *but* light and cheerful.

This is definitely a topic I would like to skip over. However, I would be doing you a disservice if I did not spend time here. With all sensitivity, I understand your loss may be very recent, yet here I am bringing up the topic and the possibility that you may go through another breakup in the future.

Hang in there with me. We will get through this. If you are thinking *no way* am I going through that again, I completely understand. This topic might be all too fresh and raw for you. I get it. Remember, I have been there. I have been there so much that I made "no dating" my New Years resolution one year! I have genuinely been to the point of being *done*.

So even if you're not ready yet, one day you will likely heal and desire companionship. Your mind will process. Your heart will mend. And you will want for a partner again. That's my hope for you. I hope you begin to date and find a rewarding relationship ahead. In your process of seeking, I also know the road can get bumpy. Realistically, dating is a risk with the heart and there may be times it will not work out. If or when that happens, please know it happens to the best of us and you *will* get through it.

I have been there and I know the hurt all too well. The first time it happened to me, I was two and a half years into the relationship. A relationship that was so solid we had talked about marriage. If that wasn't enough, it was also Valentine's weekend *and* it happened over the phone.

It was nearly 7pm that Saturday night when I called him to find out why he had not called me yet. First things first, though... He noticed I sounded scratchy and said he had Nyquil if I wanted it. *Umm, no thank you. I was calling to find out why you hadn't called me yet...* To which he simply replied he was "not feeling comfortable about this relationship."

Ohh, was that your plan – to break up before, or after, you were going to give me the Nyquil? And I guess that means we're not getting married now. I'm confused. And did you inform the kids? Who, by the way, have not been without me in two and a half years and are probably wondering where I am??

It hurt horribly. I lost the man I loved. I lost my hope of being remarried. And I lost two young children who I loved like my own. I was beyond crushed at losing them. One day shortly after, I was feeling so overwhelmed with sadness, I literally had to pull over and then got sick on the side of the road.

Then, if dealing with all of the hurt itself was not enough, I also had to handle the social aspect of the breakup. We were a part of the same singles group at church which meant each Sunday, I walked alone to our class and sat on the opposite side of the room. Awkward. Crushed. Lonely. Embarrassed.

Don's Advice

At that time, I worked with a great group of people – all about ten years older *and wiser* than me. We used to go out every Wednesday after work, and one of those nights I remember telling my boss's husband about my breakup. He said, "Do you know what you're supposed to do when that happens?" "No," I replied. Then he explained to me, "You go home in your living room and have yourself a good long cry. Then, you open the front door and walk outside to your yard. You look up and throw your hands to the sky and yell, 'NEXT!!'"

I can't say that I followed Don's advice exactly; however, I did capture the gist of what he was saying. You grieve, and it's important to do that. You accept what happened. Then, you don't stay down. You pull yourself up. You don't feel inadequate about yourself, because you are fully adequate just as you are.

You don't look back. You don't keep your eyes on the rearview mirror. You can't drive forward that way.

You look through the windshield. You look ahead. The windshield has the better view. There's the whole world in front of you. You get yourself back out there. That person robbed you of a relationship. They don't, however, deserve to rob your joy and your future opportunities.

The Art of Breaking Up

I wish I could say that first experience was the worst breakup I have ever had. Unfortunately (or perhaps fortunately depending on how you look at it), I have had others. I've been cheated on. I even had an engagement broken once. Most were without warning, without long conversation. Some were cold and sterile. Some were hurtful. And then some of them... I initiated.

When something ends, it is not always the other person causing the ending. Sometimes things simply don't work out or you learn in the dating process you are not as compatible as it first appeared. Whatever the reason, relationships sometimes take a different turn and there comes a point when a decision gets made to end it.

Even though it can be sad, disappointing, or hurtful to break up a relationship, the actual conversation can be handled in such a way to help minimize these emotions. If (when) you get to this place, treat the decision and conversation with honesty – starting with yourself. If you are truly not happy or don't want to continue dating for whatever reason, face that reality and address it as soon as possible. Leading someone on or dragging out the decision will only make the end more difficult, *for both of you.*

When you do happen to be the one desiring the break, please be considerate. If you are not happy, do your best to put yourself in the other person's shoes. You can be fully honest and direct while still being kind! Whether you have the conversation in person (recommended) or over the phone, it is always best to actually speak to them. If they still want to be friends and you're good with that, that is completely fine. I have an ex like that. It was a sad breakup, but as time went on, we realized our core values were simply too different. Total respect for each other, just not good for a partnership. At the same time, if you don't want to continue a friendship level with the person, it is fine to tell them you would rather move on completely. If that's your style, there is no apology needed! As Neil put it, breaking up *can* be hard to do; however, with a little thought and preparation, you can have a mature interaction to respectfully close that specific chapter of your life and move forward.

Depending on the situation and the one doing the breaking up, anger and frustration can also play a big part of your emotions. However, even if you want to pull out the Louisville Slugger, take a pause and consider the consequences. If someone has done you wrong, rest assured, their character will eventually be revealed. Taking the high road has a satisfaction all its own. Have you ever heard this saying? *Chickens come home to roost.* One day that person will get their own.

I also try to live by the principle in Romans 12, where we are encouraged to not repay evil when someone has done us evil. And, as much as we possibly can, we should try to live peacefully with everyone. Then I let God handle the rest because the next verse reminds me that vengeance belongs to the Lord (not me), and *He* will handle the repayment! – That definitely works for me. *I like that verse.* It's my job to do what's right and then I trust God for the justice on my behalf. I may never see it, and I'm okay with that. When I do the right thing, I walk with the clear conscience and can sleep at night with my good character.

The Rear View Mirror

And then this happens. You had a relationship. Things went off course. It ended. Whether it ended with graciousness, or without, it ended. Now you're starting over, navigating your single life *again*. It isn't great but you're doing okay. You are moving forward. All the world is in front of you. You've got a beautiful view out the windshield and life can take you anywhere now!

Days pass. Maybe weeks. The evenings are getting long. The house is quiet. Emotions are beginning to hit. Then it happens. You pull your eyes off the windshield and take a peek in the rear view mirror. You check for responses on your social media. You sneek a glance at his posts. Is there a new female in his selfies? You stop by the ice cream shop; it's not the same without him. You see something on TV that makes you laugh and you want to text him. You look again, he hasn't called to say he's changed his mind. Was it really that bad? Is he feeling the same way? It's late at night. You miss his voice.

Lady Antebellum had a song that emotionally captures this *rear view mirror* moment. It's the wee hours, she's missing him, he's missing her. They're both singing, *I need you now.* Do you call? After all, you have a comfort level together. Maybe he's feeling the same way and has a fear about calling you. You know each other. Should you try to go back? What's the best thing??

> The BEST thing? The best thing is for you to take a deep breath. – Maybe glance in Chapter 14 to distract yourself.

Personally, this is a decision only *you* can make. I know those first weeks or even months can be horribly difficult. I have been there and I know how real and hard the transition can be after a breakup.

While there is no right or wrong answer to your decision. There are some words of wisdom I can certainly pass along to you! I highly encourage you to take out your journal, write your thoughts, and look at them on paper. Sometimes that exercise alone will give you your answer. Talking with a good friend, a pastor, or counselor will also help you process. More than anything, this would be a good time to reflect on the relationship you had and get honest with yourself. What is it you would like in a relationship? There was something lacking that is highly important to you.

I wish I'd had this advice many many years ago. I had a relationship that ended. Some time later we got back together. Some time after that we broke up. And this pattern continued. I dated in between for lengthy periods. Yet I somehow ended back with this one man time and again.

We originally had plans to marry (obviously that never happened). He knew I wanted to be married. In our final round of dating, which lasted seven years, I finally got to the point where I had to face it. Marriage was not going to happen. Although I loved him dearly, the love was not reciprocated. I had to make a decision to say *enough*. I asked for a conversation with him so we could talk about it. I figured we would hit our normal walking trail and come to some kind of cordial decision. That option, however, did not happen. Coldly, the entire conversation took place over the phone, and our decades of relationship ended in 5 minutes. I was outside on a sidewalk. Getting ready for my hair appointment. He wouldn't even agree to meet with me to talk. He ended it. Our 21-year history. In five minutes.

I later learned he got engaged to someone else *7 days* after we broke up. The night I discovered that on social media, I literally could not breathe.

I'm not telling this story to say getting back together with someone is right or wrong. I am, however, strongly encouraging you to evaluate what a relationship means to you and if the relationship will meet your needs. I'm a nice person. I was loyal. I did nothing wrong and I did not deserve that. I felt as though nearly a decade of my life had been robbed. I wish I would have evaluated sooner.

You have desires and dreams for your relationships. You deserve to have those. You deserve to be loved and respected. The give and take in a partnership goes both ways. If your desires or dreams were not respected, please consider if it is really worth looking in that rear view mirror.

There is so much life ahead for you. I would hate for you to miss it while you're glancing at what is completely behind you. You may not see it at first. However, if you put yourself in drive and look ahead, there is a world out there waiting for you. New opportunities. New relationships. A new start.

> If I could encourage you in one single thing, it would be to keep positive and look ahead!

The Windshield

The interesting thing about windshields and rear view mirrors is that they both serve a purpose to ensure a safe, enjoyable journey wherever your current road is taking you. The rear view is there if you need to shift lanes. *Is anything behind me that's in my way?* The rear view mirror can tell you something from behind is approaching fast; it signals a danger! (For us ladies it can also be used to put on make-up, and that doesn't really go with my analogy here, so we'll stick with the driving principles.) While these rear view safety functions are extremely important, they are NOT designed to be your sole focus when you're driving forward! They are a *guide*, a *help*.

Think also how it would be if you had a passenger in the front seat with you. If you are the driver and you're constantly telling them about the view you're seeing behind you, well that would be a little awkward – and strange, honestly. Or, if you continued to point out the guys in the crazy cars over your shoulder?? Okay, first, your passenger is probably *not* going to feel very safe with you because your focus is on what's *behind* not what's in front of you! Accident waiting to happen, I might say. You're not giving priority to what's right in front of you. And on the common sense side, if you are constantly talking about things that are behind or things they can't see, that is both boring and quite annoying!

Pardon the pun, but are you following me here?? The windshield is your future, it's what is in front of you. It's your potential. Your current relationship. And the rear view mirror? That is your past. Your past relationships. Your past mistakes. Your life that is *behind* you. Can it be helpful? Yes. We can learn from what's behind us. But should it consume our journey forward? No! Please, no.

To begin with, your new partner will not feel comfortable if your focus is on your past. Frankly, they will get bored and annoyed if that is a constant in your conversations. Focus on what is in front of you. Focus on what's coming ahead.

With a windshield priority, then, is a rear view mirror even necessary? Oh, yes! You use what's behind to guide you. Notice I said, "You" use it to guide you. The rear view? Your past? It is a guide for you, *not a conversation piece!* Of course you take your past experiences and evaluate them. Pick them apart. Go back to those red flags and process why you overlooked them. Set new boundaries for yourself. Create new standards. Add new lines to your Top Ten list. Remove the items that didn't work for you. And when you're finished?? Dim the cabin lights, put yourself in drive, and move forward to new scenery!

Whatever happened in your past relationship is *in the past.* You will do yourself a favor to leave it there. The past is good for learning and adjusting. Once you've done that, it will be time to move on. Whatever happened, however horrid it was, the best thing you can do is acknowledge that you had a bad experience and consider what you can do in the future to avoid getting into that situation again.

Not only will this evaluation aid you going forward, it will be imperative for your future. When you start a new relationship, let it be a *new* relationship. If you constantly compare or dredge up your former partner, well, no one wants to hear that over and over again. Of course there will be some discussion of your past when you meet someone new; it's important to learn where someone has come from. After those initial conversations, however, be done and enjoy what's in front of you!

Enjoy the Journey

When you experience a break or any type of loss from a relationship, the process of reflection and growth will be one of the best things you can do for yourself. That will be the exercise that sets you up for success in your future. That initial future, however, will likely start out as a solo journey. When we've been hurt, we have little desire to jump back into dating again. When we've suffered a sad loss, it's too hard to comprehend being with another person. Regardless of the reason, our new journeys typically begin alone.

I titled this section, *Enjoy the Journey*, and I know you may be saying, "Michelle, there is no joy in this journey." You very strongly may not *want* to enjoy this journey. Maybe you can accept the windshield exercise and agree that is probably a smart move, but to enjoy being *single again*? Or single again, *again??* How does anyone enjoy that?

Well, here are your alternatives: Learn to enjoy your journey or... okay then, *don't!* It's your choice. Be sad. Be alone. Withdraw. Stay in bed. Feel sorry for yourself. Replay the history. Complain to your friends. Be bitter. Be depressed. Gain weight. Cry. Regret. Sleep in. Stay home. You are the one who controls what happens now.

Or – you can learn to enjoy this stage of your journey. If you need help doing that, it is okay to get help! Find a good counselor or Life Coach. I do highly encourage you to find one who will help you grieve and move forward to the point where you no longer need them. Note, if you take this step and you *don't* see yourself progressing, please find someone new. A counselor should not hold you down. If you need to dig deep and process what you experienced, I completely understand that. However, they should be leading you to a turning point where you see yourself growing stronger. If you take that step and you notice a period of time later that you are still dwelling on the past, please *please* find someone new.

Life is too short to let the past consume your life away. I have had more twists and knocks in relationships than there are pages for this book. Horrible twists and knocks. What is surprising to me, though, I had actually forgotten about some of them until I was typing these last paragraphs! How did I write nearly this entire book and completely forget some of those experiences? I realize now why that happened. Two main reasons: First, I had incredible help getting through one of them. Then, over time I have learned to accept that sometimes bad things happen... and those times do not define me! I could sulk. I could judge. I could think all men are horrible. And what good would that do me? That would be giving my power and joy over to someone who is not worthy of my power *or* my joy! (*And not all men are horrible, by the way.*)

So we drop the past which has served its purpose.
Now we drive forward. Looking forward.
Looking ahead to the good in front of us.

This new section of your life map may find you driving solo for a number of miles. And this may just be a special time in your life to step back and enjoy the moment! This is a period where your time is well, *your* time! Being alone definitely has its advantages. It's a time where you can find positive things to do for yourself and for others in your world. In chapters 14 and 15, (the fun I've been waiting for), you will find ideas and tips I've learned along this journey to treat myself, encourage myself, and preserve my "self". Making the decision to step outside and throw my hands to the sky was some of the best advice I've ever listened to.

I never finished telling you what happened that night of my first big breakup... I was crushed beyond belief. After I hung up the phone, I immediately called my best friend, crying my eyes out. She heard my tears and asked what was wrong. Between sobs, all I could say was, "John broke up with me." She replied back, "Ohhh, I am so sorry. – Listen, we're getting ready to go out for karaoke. Why don't you just come on with us?!" Silence. Big sniffle. Pause. ...."Okay."

I had never been out for karaoke a day in my life. But I put my jacket on, headed across town, and spent that first solo night having fun with my best friends. My first windshield moment. #Priceless.

NEXT STEPS

Something to think about...

Being honest with yourself, would you say you spend more time in the rear view mirror or looking out the windshield?

Something to move forward...

Resolve to tuck the past in its appropriate place. Grieve. Learn. Grow. Seek help. Move forward. Let it go. Your future self *and* your future partner will thank you!

Something to do...

In your journal, consider your past relationship. Then list traits you would like to see in your future relationship. If you're not seeking a future partner, write what changes you would like to see in yourself!

Walk outside. Throw your hands to the sky. And yell, "NEXT!"

14

Buy Flowers

Even though living alone can knock us off our feet sometimes, there are so very many things we can do to get back up, bring a little cheer to ourselves, and face this life head on. I don't care if you have to grunt, roll over, and push off all fours. You deserve to be on your feet. You deserve to smile. You are worthy of goodness, of little treats, and even big treats that make you feel special. Even if it is incredibly tough right now, you deserve a personal ray of sunshine!

If you are not used to doing nice things for yourself, this concept might sound uncomfortable. It may seem awkward or possibly not even fun. With family obligations or limited budget, you may feel guilty even considering a *treat-to-self*. I get that! The guilt is real when there are responsibilities and other priorities.

The reality is, we need moments of happiness in our lives to keep us going and to keep us emotionally balanced – and there is not always someone around to do that for us! The other reality, if we constantly pour ourselves into family and responsibilities, we will run out of fuel. When that happens, we are no good for those who need us and our responsibilities will suffer, as well. So these special things we do for ourselves, they keep us going for both our own sanity and so that we can be who we need to be for those in our world. You both require these recharge moments... *and* you deserve them!

About the List

When I got the idea for a chapter to offer easy ways to perk yourself up, the words "101 ways" immediately popped into my head. I'm slightly competitive, so I made it a goal to come up with exactly one hundred *and one* ideas for you! I am happy to say, I did it!!

I hope these ideas inspire you to create memories and ways of your own that will brighten your spirits when there is no one else there to do it for you. We all have different personalities, abilities, and budgets, so the list includes a variety of tips that are both doable and affordable for almost anyone. If anything, I hope they inspire you to create your own perk-me-up ideas!

As I was finishing the list, I realized some suggestions required a bit more thought and planning. I've separated those larger ideas into their own section. Thus, Chapter 15, *Build a Greenhouse!"*

Every one of these suggestions are personal things I have done over the years. This is not a generic list snagged from the internet or one with outrageous ideas which I wouldn't be willing to try myself. (No skydiving excursions listed... not even ziplines!) These are ideas to treat yourself special, stretch your social connections, spiff up your home, or give yourself a much deserved break.

Most of them were done on a budget, when I was working long hours, and many while I still had kids at home. Living my very ordinary life, very single again. To this day, my favorite flowers are still the $4 bunch from the grocery store and my trip locations don't have to include five stars. This is about taking a deep breath, calling a time-out, and stepping away for a recharge. While these ideas are things I've personally done, this list is my wish list for you, too. These simple moments have kept me going, and I hope they inspire you to keep going, as well.

Enjoy. Venture. Relax.
Step outside your comfort zone. I did!

#1 Easy Steam Facial

I learned this trick years ago and still love it. First, find a cleanser with a wonderful spa scent. Yes, from *any* cleanser aisle! Next: Lather up, lean back, place a hot steaming washcloth over your face. (Microwaves make great steamers!). Take in a deep moist breath. Enjoy the heat, the steam in your sinuses, the aroma. Slowly exhale. Repeat. Repeat. Rinse. Relax.

#2 Grill Outside

I bought my first grill one year for Mother's Day and discovered I love grilling. It gets me outside in the fresh air, eating healthier, and bonus... No pans to clean! Super fun. Highly recommend.

#3 Drink from a Special Mug

When I make a hot drink, I like it to be an experience. Years ago I started buying souvenir mugs to save memories of trips I'd taken. Some were my own adventures, others were taken with my kids. Every day I enjoy a sweet memory of theme parks, the mountains, or shows I've seen. Find a mug that speaks your language. Then heat. Sip. Savor.

#4 Start a Hobby

Struggling with the open space in your life? This is a great time to start a hobby *of your own.* Once, after moving to a new home, I discovered I could create classy floral arrangements. (Who knew!) I even learned to paint vases to coordinate with my new decor. I then got outside and discovered I have quite the knack for landscaping! Extra bonus? An old friend flew in to teach me about plants. – Great girls trip. Learned lots. Made forever memories.

Surprise yourself and try something new! Bunco nights? Photography? Knitting? Baking? By the way, hobbies can double as a great way to make gifts!

#5 Attend a Ladies Night

Signing up for a church event alone is a bit outside my comfort zone. On one occasion, our church was having a special Ladies Night and a peer from work invited me to go with her friends. (Yes... Someone from another church invited me to go with her to *my* church!) It was inspirational and I got to hear a well-known singer. It's also a good way to meet new people or check out a new church! (More on that in Chapter 15.)

#6 Have a Yard Sale

There is not much better for the soul than to clear the clutter – and make a few bucks in the process! My go-to for decluttering is generally a thrift store drop-off; however, I once had some larger, nicer items I preferred to sell. It was much easier than I expected and came with additional benefits. By *selling* the larger items, I didn't have to worry about toting them away myself. Also, that day I met some neighbors I hadn't met previously! Great experience. New Friends. $300.

#7 Plant Herbs

While I am improving, I have to admit I do NOT have a green thumb. I say that to say, *if I can do this, you can, too!* I once got the idea to plant herbs. I'm not sure what I thought I was going to do with them exactly but, nonetheless, I bought them. It was an easy list: herbs, plastic planters, potting soil, and a rack to hang on my deck rail. Oddly enough, with just a little water, they grow like crazy! Eventually I learned I could pluck the rosemary to grill on my chicken, and the basil is addicting with mozzarella and cherry tomatoes on toasted baguettes! If you won't use a lot, it might be rewarding to share with your neighbors or simply enjoy the aromas.

#8 Check Out World Market

I'm not really one to enjoy going to the store for no reason. What I do enjoy from time to time, though, is a trip to World Market. If you haven't been to one, or haven't been lately, have yourself a visit and check out the unique items. (My kids taught me they also have free coffee samples!) If you don't have a World Market, try venturing to another city to visit one and make the day an experience. Or is there another unique store you haven't tried? Pop in and see what treasures you might find. Be sure to treat yourself while you're there!

#9 Get a Library Card

When my kids were small, we made regular visits to the library. Then they grew up, life settled in, and I almost forgot about libraries. The reality is, they are a great way to enjoy your reading hobby without the expense of buying all the time. Also, I have recently discovered some libraries have used books and puzzles for sale! If you haven't tried one lately, find a rainy afternoon and go have yourself a visit.

#10 Foot Spa on the Counter

Sometimes life is simply too busy or the budget too tight to consider full spa visits. Those seasons of life, however, never stopped me from wanting a pampered experience. Not to worry; I discovered a way to make my own spa experience!

First, put on relaxing music. Next, light candles in your bathroom. Place fluffy towels around and gently slip up onto your counter. Swing your feet into the sink and fill with steamy water and soapy bubbles. (I literally pump my hand soap, but feel free to go all out!) Add scented oils and have a relaxing drink to enhance the experience. Feel free to rub your aching feet or merely enjoy the quiet moment. When you're finished, rinse with hot water, pat your feet dry, rub with cream, and slip under the covers. Mmmm.

#11 Experiment with New Recipes

One of the advantages of being single is the freedom to cook and eat foods a partner maybe didn't enjoy. Is there a type of food or recipe you've wanted to test? Now is your time! Years ago, I logged in to the All Recipes site, and to this day that is my go-to. I even have a 3-ring binder where I've printed and saved winners over the years. Give your taste buds a treat. – *Bon Appétit!*

#12 Take Yourself to Dinner

If there is no one taking you on a date, there is no need to miss out on having someone cook for you! If it feels awkward, remember, people don't know that you're not traveling for business. When I do this, I take a book to read or paper to write. As I was working on this chapter, I had a delicious lunch-with-self at an outdoor café while traveling. I focused on the food and the moment. It was wonderful!

#13 Develop a New Night Ritual

Starting something new gives your brain moments of allowing you to focus on what you're doing rather than on your situation. Creating a night routine that's *yours* will give you a sense of identity. And depending on what you choose, it could be a solid way to tell your brain it's time to wind down and rest well. My daughter once created a tradition of drinking tea in the evening. This both helped her relax, and also gave her a new hobby! One of my rituals is closing the blinds. As simple as that sounds, it's *my thing* to do at night. I think it's subconsciously my way of saying the day is over and it's time for me to shut down, too. It's simple, yet special, and makes me feel good to have a routine that's mine, not attached to anyone else.

#14 Walk in the Park

As you're seeing, not every perk-up has to be monumental. Finding a park with a walking trail is a perfect example. It gives you fresh air, vitamin D, oxygen for your brain, quiet time to reflect, exercise, and people to say hello along the way. Enough said.

#15 Buy Yourself an Ice Cream Cone

Nothing says *cheer up* quite like an ice cream cone. For an added twist, try a new flavor you've never had before. Or better yet, how about a whole new ice cream shop?! Treat yourself! Enjoy.

#16 Organize Your Photos

Whether you still have printed photos stashed in your cabinets or you've topped the thousands number in your cell phone, taking a day to clear out and organize will give you a refreshing sense of accomplishment – as well as extra space! Keep a box of tissues handy for the memories. Sadness is okay. Once you're finished, though, you will have all those memories placed exactly where you want them.

#17 Sips & Strokes

Even if you don't have artistic bones in your body, canvas and acrylic paints are fairly forgiving. One idea is to go to a Paint & Sip class where you bring your own beverage and make an evening of it.

It's also relaxing to paint at home! Start with a few simple items from your local craft store. I stash my supplies in a girly tool box and use a disposable plastic table cloth when I want to play with paints. Additional idea: Invite some girlfriends over for your own Sips & Strokes party! Then hang your handiwork... or use for a white elephant if it's really bad!

#18 Sonic Drive-in

Do you have a Sonic in town? Or any other drive-in type root beer stand? These are a great way to treat yourself without breaking the bank or feeling awkward about being seen eating alone. Having a lazy self-conscious day? Drive in and enjoy that chili dog!

#19 Movie & Popcorn Night

If you need permission to slow yourself down and have a play night, here you go. Stick that popcorn bag in the microwave... or treat yourself to a popcorn store! Throw on comfy jammies. Pull up your go-to movie genre or an old fav. Add soda. Have fun!

#20 Take a Bubble Bath

I am aware this is not the most original suggestion. I wanted to add it, though, in case you needed a reminder. From time to time, give yourself a hot sudsy bubbly kind of break. Add relaxing music, candles, and drink of your choice. Soak your worries away!

#21 Start a Collection

Being alone often holds moments when you feel slightly stir crazy. If you find yourself getting bored, start a collection of some kind! It gives you something to do with your time, especially if you feel the need to get out of the house. It can be simple. I used to collect small rocks of places I'd been, including local hiking treks. I de-ocrated with a cylinder vase on my dresser! Now I collect seashells and use them in my décor!

#22 Put Together a Jigsaw Puzzle

If you have not done this or not done one in awhile, this is an ideal way to ease your mind of your worries. If the task seems daunting or you're not sure it's your thing, start small with 300 pieces. I generally have a 1,000 piece on my dining room table. When I'm finished, I place my basket of vines on it and it becomes part of the center piece. Be careful, though. They can become an addiction!

#23 Hors d'Oeuvres Night

You do not need a group of people to enjoy an evening of special hors d'oeuvres! One of my very favorite ways to spoil myself is with a purchase of seafood salad from Publix. No prep required! It works on fancy crackers as well as clubs. I also have an amazing, easy meatball recipe. Put together your favorite fancies. Add drink. Candles. Music. Deck or patio. Tiki torches. Mmm, special evening to self.

#24 Decorate Your Patio

Every season, I enjoy getting myself a treat for the deck or patio. Maybe you'll choose a décor piece or new cushions? My favorite is finding a unique tropical-looking plant for my big ceramic pot. Some of my go-to plants are the Red Mandevillas or anything with a pop of orange!

#25 Download an App

I thought phone games were only for young hipsters, but I have since seen all kinds of people playing when I've traveled. If you haven't yet tried one, visit your app store! They're a great way to get your mind off things. p.s. Set a timer!

#26 Volunteer at a Nursing Home

One way to get unstuck from your rut is to give of yourself to others. Contact the Activities Director of your local nursing home for ideas. It's a rewarding experience and the staff will be grateful!

#27 Bake Yourself a Cake or Cookies

There's nothing like getting out the mixing bowl and whipping up a chocolatey dessert *for yourself*. If you live alone, don't underestimate the ability to consume an entire cake on your own! If you must be disciplined, chocolate chip cookies do just fine in the freezer!

#28 Take a Downtown Stroll

An easy way to snag a *social* fix is to take yourself downtown. When's the last time you shopped a boutique? Go try on a new style! Then be sure to slip into the candy shop to splurge on a truffle. And while you're out 'n about, smile at a stranger!

#29 Try a New Coffee Spot or Coffee Drink

I will always remember my first trip into a Starbucks. It took less than 5 seconds to realize I had no idea what I was doing. Thankfully, the person in front of me ordered a Caramel Macchiato. That sounded good so I ordered one, too! All these years later, I still have no idea what any of those drinks are, but it always makes me feel special to order a Caramel Macchiato in whichever coffee shop I take myself. Sip – Savor – Enjoy

#30 Buy a Fire Pit

One of my fav purchases was investing in a small fire pit from the home improvement store. *If I can do it, you can, too!* If you're not a fire pro, they do make logs you simply light and they'll burn for hours! Some of my best evenings were spent enjoying a drink, the fire, tiki torches, and my serene back yard. Light a log and relax!

#31 Get a Free Make-over

When is the last time you took yourself to the mall or large department store? Plan your next visit with a call in advance to schedule a make-over! If you can't afford a purchase, simply tell them you want to wear your new look for a day before deciding. – Be sure to stop by the earrings and purses while you're there!

#32 Plant Flowers

Flowers are an easy way to brighten your day and they are truly easy. Needed: Small shovel, flowers, potting soil. (Pot optional.) Instructions: Dig, plant, sprinkle, pat, water. When all else fails, try a hanging basket! Water every 1-2 days. Petunias are almost foolproof.

#33 Replace Your Bedspread!

I am all about creating the bedroom into your own private haven. Recently I had a bedspread that had truly met its last day. I found the perfect bed set on a half-price sale day. I then repurposed one of my pillows, snagged a second from another bed, and yet a third from part of my décor. Every single day this room brings me peace, and everyone who sees it remarks how calming it is. Total cost? Priceless.

#34 Read a Novel Whenever You Want

One of the benefits of living alone is your flexibility. Reading is definitely a time filler and there's no one to tell you to turn out the light! Add a treat for yourself and buy a new bookmark! Another treat? Start book trading with your bestie and your hairstylist!

#35 Try a New Kitchen Gadget

Have you ventured into the kitchen section of the department store lately? One of my favorite things to do is check out what new creative gadgets are out there. Some of my all-time favs I use almost daily: My sandwich knife which allows me to slice *and* spread! Toaster tongs – No more burned fingers! My rubber spoontulas? I now have three!

#36 Visit a Museum

This is a terrific idea to slip away for a day focused elsewhere than your situation. You may be surprised to find museums near your home. I recently discovered an incredible museum 30 minutes away. Who knew!

#37 Subscribe to a Magazine

How fun is it to get something in the mail besides advertisements?! Years ago, when my schedule was rather chaotic, I discovered *Real Simple*. At the time, my life was in much need for slowing down and it was such a mail treat on magazine day!

#38 Day of Bargain Shopping

While I am not the most enthusiastic shopper in the store, I do enjoy a day trip to the outlet mall! Go have yourself a little fun checking out bargains. – Be sure to take a few extra bucks for a snack.

#39 Buy Flowers

Having a down day? Take yourself to the grocery store and cheer yourself up in the floral department. My all time favorites – Orange Queen Alstroemeria.

Go love on yourself!

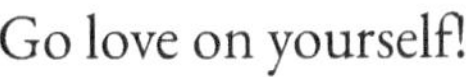

#40 Design a Memory Board

A pet peeve of mine is saving items as memories and stuffing them into a dark box, never to be seen again. What is the point?! My kids once gave me the idea to hot glue square sheets of cork onto the plastic cover of a framed poster picture. This gave me a decorative cork board with a nice frame!

I hung the board in my bonus room. Each time we went somewhere special, I tacked our memories onto it. Tickets, wristbands, even 3D glasses. – So meaningful and a fun conversation piece!

#41 Create Yourself a Gourmet Meal

Treat yourself to a gourmet dinner. Cooking alone does not have to be a quick cheap fix. Buy yourself a small fresh piece of steak. (Hopefully you have the grill I suggested.) Add a colorful salad, loaded potato, and background music with candles perhaps??

Being alone does not mean we have to miss out. Put on your Master Chef apron and see where it takes you. When my family is gone on Thanksgiving, I actually prepare an *entire* full-size Thanksgiving dinner just for me. – Complete with pumpkin pie and Macy's parade! Yum.

#42 Sign Up for Car Radio Service

A funny memory I have of my mom was her questioning, "Why would you PAY for radio in your car when you can have it for free?!" Ha, she did not understand all the options or the ad-free music. At one tough point of my career, Joel Osteen on XM (and journaling) was the *only thing* that got me through. Give it a try with a free trial!

#43 A Fresh Set of Dish Towels

Have your dish towels seen better days? Searching for a new set is a great reason for a little shopping spree. They're also an easy, inexpensive way to brighten your mood in the kitchen!

#44 Organize Your Junk Drawer

Organizing is *not* a chore! Years ago I read Sandra Felton's, *The Messies Manual*. I learned two ideas I have lived by for decades: 1) Eliminate and concentrate, and 2) Is there a place for everything and everything in its place.

Three piles: Keep. Toss. Donate. One result: Happiness.

#45 Plant a Garden or Tomato Plant

Vegetable gardens are a great way to get your mind on something productive – and so rewarding when you get to eat what you've grown! If you are limited on space (or gardening skills), cherry tomato plants are super easy with a quick return on your investment! Great for salads, sandwiches, or a bruschetta night!

#46 Wine Tasting

I learned years ago that there is more to wine drinking than intoxication. The art of wine is really interesting. A fun evening is to stop by a free wine tasting. Sample and learn. Be responsible. Cheers!

#47 Start a Journal

If you've not done this, I highly encourage you. This is a healthy way to sort your thoughts and set goals for yourself. You can then watch your progress – or observe the obstacles preventing you from moving forward. My journals demonstrated dead ends I was facing and the resulting decisions that had to be made. I personally love the fitlosophy fitspiration journal!

#48 Refresh Your Bathroom

This is where you prep your days and wind down your nights. What message is your bathroom speaking to you? Is it, *My world is put together ready for my entrance!* Or is it saying, *My life is chaotic and messy!* You can change that message with a simple trip to a home goods store. Try a new shower curtain, a few organizer baskets, a wall shelf, or even a tasteful hand towel. What about painting an accent wall with your leftover bedroom paint?! Enjoy your makeover!

#49 Snuggle Under a New Blanket

Sometimes the best way to feel better is to sink and hide for a spell. I found the fluffiest, snuggliest blanket at Target. Mmm, soft suede feel on one side, thick furry on the other. I don't care if I live in Florida (or my age), this is my go-to and my world becomes right.

#50 Schedule a Massage

When is the last time you got truly pampered? Well, it's time now! If this is new for you, several places have different prices and options. This is also a great gift suggestion for your family.

#51 Buy a Scratch-Off

For the record, I do *not* support serious gambling. This perk idea is merely entertainment! For a little post-grocery-shopping fun, try your luck with a $2 scratch-off. The cards with a game and lots of spaces will last longer and provide more of that *Did-I-Win* anticipation. Bonus idea: These make great gift stuffers *and* they support education or other causes in your home state!

#52 Notes to Self or to a Friend

Think of 5 positive statements about yourself or 5 goals you'd like to achieve. Write them on sticky notes and place in random areas around your home. When you see them, read aloud. Smile. It might sound silly, but I'd rather you sound silly with self motivation than sad with emptiness. Not up for this one? Then how about mailing an old-fashioned handwritten letter to bring cheer to a friend?!

#53 Catch a Game at a Sports Bar

If there's a big game coming on and you want to share the excitement, there are plenty of sports restaurants with big screens. Toss on your jersey, enjoy the comradery, top it off with an order of wings!

#54 Go Antiquing

When's the last time you visited an antique store? Even if this is *not* your thing, it's interesting to take a trip down memory lane. Take an afternoon to experience a blast from the past.

#55 Listen to Music

Not just any old music or your favorite genre, venture out to a new station! I discovered I love putting on our cable *Tropicales* channel. Bonus: I burn more calories cleaning with my salsa moves!

#56 Drive Somewhere Without a Plan

I did this when my kids were young and it's still an adventure. You'll discover neat small towns, quaint shops, and beautiful countryside. Throw your car in drive and caution to the wind for a day!

#57 Relax on Your Porch or Patio

Sometimes perking yourself up can come by simply slowing yourself down. Sitting outside allows time to breathe, reflect, read, or dream. I added 2 white rockers to my front porch years ago. In the spring, pot a new plant or add a glass of lemonsade to the experience!

#58 Buy Fresh Pillows

Living room or bedroom, new pillows are a definite pick-me-up! A fresh toss on the sofa will cheer up your down time. Or a new fluff under your head tonight? Your body will thank you tomorrow.

#59 Netflix Binge Weekend

A planned, private binge *staycation* can be quite the fun weekend. Make sure you have ample snack food and, if you want to stay in your PJs for two days... who will know?! My favorite binges are the mini-series. Just remember, this idea is for a *weekend*, not a habit!

#60 Get Your Nails Done

If you're not in the routine of getting your nails done, consider this your pampering-of-choice. Gel will last weeks and weeks. My former tech, Linn, asked me to help her improve her English. We had fun and I made a friend in the process!

#61 Meander in a Book Store

Even if you live a bit away, it might be worth the drive to enjoy a couple hours at a book store. Sip a special drink, browse novels, check out cookbooks, dream in the travel section, find a new journal, buy a puzzle, spoil yourself with a small gift. So much to treasure.

#62 Walk the Neighborhood

I wear a sport watch and have charted myself a one-mile path. Along that mile, I've met the nicest neighbors (and puppies) I would not have known otherwise. Walking is good for your heart *and* soul!

#63 Frame a Picture

I'm not one to have many photos around the house, but I do have a few memorable moments blended into my décor. A picture of my kids as teens walking toward a mountain on a special trip. The last group picture with my mom and all of us girls. An adorable photo of my granddaughter at age one, wrapped in a beach towel, peeking over my shoulder. All impromptu moments. And all of them still warm my heart when I see them. Frame a special memory where you'll be able to easily find a smile and warm feeling.

#64 Check Out the Farmer's Market

Many towns have a Farmer's Market or Festivals. This is a fun opportunity to get outside, find fresh vegetables, try a new piece of jewelry, or spoil yourself with a home-baked treat. Explore. Enjoy!

#65 Make Dessert Concoctions

This is definitely one of my favorite perk-up suggestions! Creating parfaits with sliced fruit and whip cream. Add anything crushed like Oreos or nuts or graham crackers. Drizzle syrups. Oh the endless possibilities. Create. Indulge. Reap the satisfaction!

NEXT STEPS

Something to think about...

Are you making time to treat yourself with special moments that will lift your spirits? If not, *why not?*

Something to move forward...

Who suffers when you get tired, sad, or frustrated? Family? A friend? You?? Commit to re-fueling yourself.

Something to do...

Pick one or two items from this chapter and go put them on your calendar. Next month... Repeat!

What's your favorite kind of flower?

15

Build a Greenhouse!

> There are those quick times in our everyday life when we need to stop by the grocery store and lift our spirits with a colorful bouquet... There are other times in life when we simply need to build a whole greenhouse!

I am speaking rather metaphorically here to continue from the last chapter *Buy Flowers*; however, if you have a green thumb, this truly is NOT so far-fetched. Did you know you can order a 6'x6' greenhouse through Wayfair for under $300?! If you're an avid gardener, you might actually consider putting a greenhouse purchase on your own list of 101 ways to perk yourself up!

Metaphorically then, we have times in our everyday life when a fresh-bouquet-experience will give us that quick boost we need. And then we have those not-so-everyday times of life. Those periods when we're desiring more. Wanting more for ourselves. Truly needing more. Whether it's an experience, a lifestyle change, or an accomplishment we want to achieve. There's a desire gnawing at us, telling us there's yet more for our life. *It's bigger than a bouquet.*

Initially, these 36 remaining ideas were tucked in the last chapter and they completed my goal of offering you 101 different ways to perk yourself up. I realized, though, while these last 36 definitely *will* perk you up, they are somewhat bigger ideas. And bigger ideas require bigger planning, budgeting, scheduling, and preparing. They are activities and actions you'll want to consider and perhaps research. For that reason, I have broken them into their own group here so you can slow down while we dream together and truly consider, "What would I like to do? How would I like my life to change? What is something I want to do for myself that I've not had the flexibility or confidence to attempt?"

I cannot stress enough, if we are constantly pouring ourselves into family and responsibilities, we *will* run out, dry up, and wither. When that happens, we are no good to our kids or friends, and our responsibilities will suffer, as well. So you see, this list, these special things we might do for ourselves. They are not just for fun, they are part of our surviving – and I might add, our *thriving*. They will revive you and keep you who you need to be, not only for yourself, but also for those in your world who need you.

If you think bigger things are not possible for you, please block those thoughts! With a pinch of creativity and a little exploring, you'll be surprised what you are capable of. *Honestly, I have to admit I would have thought building a greenhouse was out of reach.*

All I had to do was a little research and I discovered even a greenhouse is possible! Whatever greenhouse dream you might have, don't dismiss the idea so quickly. Dreams and goals give us energy and something to work toward.

It's time to acknowledge that you control your circumstances, they do not control you. It's time to overcome any defeating voices and move forward. It is healthy to accept that, yes, single life is different. You may not like it. You may not have wanted this. The reality is, you are here. You have found yourself on this road, and it is time to take the healthy path. The path that both acknowledges the loss and chooses to make positive decisions. The path where you value yourself. The road that acknowledges, "I have worth." The road that allows you to offer good things to your life. You can make a choice to be a *victor* in your circumstances, rather than a *victim*.

The sooner you make this choice, the sooner you begin to create a new version of yourself. A version of you who has self-worth, new experiences, and accomplishments. This is not a motivational speech and neither is it far fetched! My list is not extravagant; it's just a little more involved than the $4 Publix bouquet. I consider myself quite ordinary and I have done all of these. Most on a budget; some outside my comfort zone! But they all added incredible quality to my single life. I hope they trigger ideas for you. And I hope they perk up your life as much as they did mine.

Dream. Plan. Be Brave.

#66 Develop New Eating Habits

There are multiple benefits in changing or improving your way of eating, and this is an opportune time to experiment with new cuisine! Better choices will help reduce weight, improve heart health, and uplift your emotions. Whether you are shifting to low carb or want to have more ethnic food in your meals, new habits are fun and give you something to look forward to.

Years ago, I went through a program where I learned to eat healthier. The initial cost was around $300, and I can say it was one of the best investments I have ever made! I learned so much and now know how to easily keep my body looking and feeling healthy. Clear your shelves! It's time to replace your food items with healthy options or the ethnic fare you've been wanting to try.

Feel great– Have fun!

#67 Hit a Hiking Trail

There is taking a walk... and then there is hiking a trail! This is one of my favorite things to do. Spending a day on a trail is a great way to clear your head, get fresh air, challenge the muscles, get a little dirty, and enjoy God's nature. When I lived in Tennessee, I loved hiking Radnor Lake. Sometimes I would carry my journal to the top of Ganier Ridge and sit for awhile sorting my thoughts. It was both physically and mentally refreshing.

I've also hiked other locations in the state, as well as the Rockies of Colorado. We have 88,000 miles of hiking trails in the U.S. Do your research and plan a day *or an entire trip!* Remember to pack comfortable shoes, healthy snacks, and water!

– Do your body good.

#68 Host a Party

One holiday season while chatting with neighbors, I decided to host an open house for our cul-de-sac so we could get to know each other better. This is not something I'd be brave enough to do myself and was grateful to have one of the neighbor girls volunteer to make (and deliver!) the invitations. While I provided the core of the food and drinks, everyone was encouraged to bring their favorite party food. Such a fun way to get to know neighbors I had not yet met. *Another year, I hosted our holiday office party!*

Plan your event carefully. My creativity is a gift and a curse at the same time. I once offered to throw a birthday party for my neighbor's daughter. One idea led to another, and I'm certain that party cost me well over $200! It was incredibly fun and worth it. Just be mindful those tiny details add up. No doubt though, parties are great ways to add extra social fun to your life without an ongoing commitment. –Cheers!

#69 Study a New Language

Even if you know you will never use it, learning a new language is fun and adds other benefits to your life. At the top of the list, it gives you a personal challenge and exercises your brain! There are various ways you can learn a different language, including taking classes, to using a simple language app like Duolingo. Even though it will take some time, you will enjoy the accomplishment and have fun trying it out with others.

I once used a program called, *Learn Spanish in Your Car* and completed the lessons during my work commutes. I learned enough phrases that I was able to begin communicating with our night cleaning crew when I worked late! Prior to that we were not able to speak with each other at all. It was fun and they, in turn, taught me even more. – ¡Buena suerte!

#70 Try a Work-out Facility or Exercise Routine

If this seems intimidating, I encourage you to give it a try! Most facilities have staff to help you learn the machines, as well as classes for beginners. It's a great way to get yourself out of the house, improve your health, and give yourself a mental boost! Years ago I would go to the Y after work a few nights a week. It was really awkward at first and, after a few weeks, I had my routine of treadmill, weights, whirlpool, sauna, and even swimming laps!!

#71 Paint a Room

If this idea sounds more like a chore rather than a perk, think again! A freshly painted room does wonders for your soul. If you're not experienced, I recommend starting with your bedroom. It will be relatively easy with no hard parts to reach or paint around. My favorite paint is Behr Marquis because it covers in one coat. I had purchased a fixer upper and the dark butterscotch master bedroom definitely required a make-over. I took that butterscotch to a cozy relaxing cottage villa in one coat and it blended beautifully with my furniture. Everyone who sees my room remarks how calming it is, *which is exactly the effect I wanted*. You can imagine the change in my frame of mind. It was a complete mood lifter. Give your personal space a makeover. – Perk up your walls *and* your spirits!

#72 Try a New Small Appliance

I've always been a decent cook. One thing I lacked, though, was fixing food outside of the basics. After I moved to a house with greater counter space, I learned how much fun I could have testing things in a toaster oven. I then got completely hooked on my panini maker. And to this day, protein shakes are a regular afternoon snack from my blender. –Splurge and gift yourself with a new kitchen toy!

#73 Take a Vacation

This one might feel way outside your comfort zone. I'm talking about vacation *by yourself.* If you want to take a trip, you may not have anyone who can go with you. Please, treat yourself anyway! After finishing my masters, I wanted to celebrate with a beach trip. There was no one to go with me and I still wanted to reward myself. Let me tell you, that was the best trip! It started with my car rental being unavailable – so they gave me an upgrade to a red convertible! THAT was fun. Then there was the discovery that I'd accidentally booked myself at a *luxury resort!*

If you're wondering how I accidentally booked a high-end resort or how I was able to afford it, allow me to step you into my shoes for a moment. I was working long hours and prepping for graduation. Not too many days before my "vacation" I realized that, in all the chaos, I had never actually *booked* my vacation! Needless-to-say, I immediately checked out one of those sites where you book cheap last minute travel. I quickly found a car to rent, as well as a hotel on the beach that fit my budget. (Whew!) Before I left, I printed the confirmation with the address, stuffed it in my bag, and off I went.

You can imagine my incredible surprise when I pulled up to a beautifully landscaped, inclined entrance, complete with a sign that read, *Valet Parking Only.* I literally double-checked the address because I thought I'd gone to the wrong location! In the resort, the walkways had piped music. My tiled shower had an opening where I could look out across the room, past the beautiful bed with its sheered canopy, and then to the terra cotta balcony overlooking the ocean. I returned from dinner the first night finding my drapes pulled, soft music playing, sheets turned down, and a teddy bear with chocolates placed on the pillows. I loved my job and children dearly; however, I have to admit I never wanted to leave that place!

As for being by myself, there was plenty to enjoy. I was able to come and go as I pleased. I scheduled a hair appointment with the salon, stayed in the sun all day, chose which restaurants I wanted for dinner, ate when I felt like it, took my time... and truly wished I could have stayed longer. That was the first of several beach trips I have taken alone. It's a wonderful opportunity to reset, reflect, and recharge. Please treat yourself at least once!

#74 Try a Local Social Group

With the changes of friendship we experience, we can find ourselves socializing less. It's important for our mental health, though, to stay active and engaged. One way to do this is through a social group. In the past, I discovered business networking opportunities with Eventbrite. I know other singles who have stayed engaged through avenues such as Meetup or Facebook Groups. If your social life is shrinking, research the different groups in your area. You'll be surprised how many other singles are out there looking for friendships, too. In chapter 5, I talked about the singles group I created for our community. Organizing that was far beyond my comfort zone! Yet all it took was for me to ask the simple question, and so many kind people stepped up to encourage me. Before that, I would never have guessed how many other singles were in my small suburb wishing for a group, as well.

Take that first step forward to meet new friends. Others are out there wishing for friendships just like you!

#75 Start a Fresh Wardrobe

One of my favorite shopping trips was a venture into Banana Republic. I had dropped some pounds and needed to update with clothes that fit more appropriately. The staff joined in and had so much fun picking out clothes and helping me learn how to dress with my new weight loss. Regardless of your reason, a new outfit is super fun. Clearance rack? Even more fun. Overall? Great confidence booster!

#76 Attend Dave Ramsey's FPU

In Chapter 7, I spoke about finances. If you have not heard of Dave Ramsey, I encourage you to get to know him. He has an amazing story and developed a program called *Financial Peace University*. Several churches conduct the 2-month course, or a virtual option is now available. I went through FPU years ago and became financially stable on my single income! A nominal fee helps cover the materials expense, and what you gain for the fee is priceless. It is very easy to understand, the lessons are interesting and meaningful, and you will develop amazing new habits. I highly highly recommend.

#77 Rip Up Carpet at 10pm

Okay, maybe you won't want to follow what I did specifically in this tip; however, it was an amazing experience. At one point, I had been looking at my living room night after night *after night* desperately wanting to scratch it and start over! One evening, I'd had enough. I literally scooted my furniture completely out of the way, including a piano that I wheeled into the kitchen. Then, I grabbed a corner and yanked and rolled that carpet right up! I'm laughing at the memory. (It's vivid.) What came next was tugging that huge roll of carpet out the front door somewhere in the 10:00p.m. hour of that drizzly, rainy night. Note, if you try this, carpet is very heavy. I had no idea, but by that point it was too late. It was a chore, yet so worth it. The next day I had a friend recommend a reasonable flooring store and, within 2 weeks, I had freshly painted walls, beautiful new furniture, and... of course, new carpet! I absolutely loved that room. One of my very best crazy ventures ever.

#78 Check Out a New Church

This is possibly a very hard decision for you to make. Even if things are awkward at your current church, it is still familiar with familiar faces, and style, and even familiar hallways. However, if there is lack of friendship, bad memories, gossip, or rumors (*I know*, humans actually go to church), it may be time to let it go! Do yourself a favor and consider finding a new place of worship which suits you better. When I made this step, it took several tries to find a church that felt like it could be my new home. I do understand the challenge of it all. The searching and visiting was not the most enjoyable part of the process; however, within a short amount of time, I grew to love where I landed even more than where I had been.

It might help if you call a church prior to your visit and speak to someone about their options for single adults in your age range. Finding a bible study group for singles, specifically older ones, will give you a core group of friends who can relate to your situation. A singles group can be a support for you, and a lift to your spirits!

Years ago I took that step and discovered a group of people who were walking in my shoes. That transition led to memories and lifelong friendships far beyond church on Sunday. Some of my favorite memories are the annual girls trips I would take with three of my best girlfriends to the Gulf Coast. Incredibly fun beach trips. Priceless memories.

#79 Volunteer in the Bistro

There is finding a new church… and then there is getting *involved* in a new church. If you live in a smaller town where there might not be a plethora of single adult bible studies, another great option to build friendships is to find an area to volunteer! I've mentioned my slightly shy streak, so you can imagine the trepidation making friends at a new church. In one of the churches, I asked about meeting single people. I was directed to Brenda, who ran the Bistro on Sundays. I not only made friends with the group working in the Bistro, it also gave me terrific opportunity to meet and interact with all kinds of people every Sunday. I can't stress enough how good it is to keep yourself engaged with volunteering. You'll have friends to share stories and good times every week! – A definite perk-up while you're doing something good for others.

#80 Attend a Business Convention

When I was in the years of building my career, I invested in attending national conventions related to my field. These were always stimulating trips where I walked away with fresh ideas, made new connections, and *bonus*, got to experience different parts of the country. I always leveraged the new knowledge to develop ideas for my career. Some of the workshops I developed were later recognized on a national level, and some of my training pieces were even used globally! If attending the conventions was not enough of a boost, the additional recognition gave me an even greater sense of accomplishment. This all took place during the time when my social and home life were quite lonely, and I was ever grateful for the amazing opportunities. I strongly encourage you to consider investing in your career. You will gain multiple wins!

#81 Buy Your Own Birthday or Christmas Presents

If you have not yet done this, you must! The holidays can be very sad and lonely when you're by yourself. (I've had plenty of them.) What I learned though, is that you can make buying your own gift an event in itself. Why should we go without presents simply because we're alone? One year, I moved slightly before the holiday season and would be completely alone for the first time at Christmas. As deliveries for my new house began to arrive, I realized I couldn't remember all I'd purchased. Then I got a funny idea to wrap the boxes and save them under my tree. I waited until Christmas Eve to open them, which was our family tradition. Let me just say, that silly idea kept me from feeling completely lost that year, and I truly had fun seeing my online shopping come to life in my new home. You deserve a gift-to-self. Go wrap one!

#82 Party on a Yacht

If you feel limited in resources or circumstances, that is no reason to think you can't have extraordinary experiences! In one of my groups, I became friends with one of the guys and helped him with visits to his mom in the nursing home. He just happened to own a yacht and, at one point, he offered to let me have a party with my friends on his boat. He took us up the river to a restaurant where we had dinner and it was simply the best day. Please never limit yourself to think those experiences are for the rich and famous. Some people are simply nice and have resources they enjoy sharing. If someone offers you a big treat, take them up on it!

#83 Go Furniture Shopping

Even if you can't afford it! You don't have to be in the market for new furniture to go see what new designs are in style. It's a good way to dream or to see how much you would need to save for that piece you discover. One of my furniture excursions was with a friend who had recently moved into a new place. It was so much fun helping them pick their furniture. Spending someone else's money? Even more fun!

#84 Annual Beach Walk

Somewhere along the way on one of my vacations, I took a long, long walk on the beach for some much needed reflection time. That walk was so beneficial, I made a commitment to do it annually. It's my one time to get away, review where my life is, and what I want to change. It is now a tradition to make sure I have that walk annually. Whether it's a beach walk or not. What tradition might you start with yourself?

#85 Become an Uber Driver

Want to make some extra cash and have opportunity to socialize?! Driving for Uber may be the ride you're looking for! One time between jobs, I *thought* I was looking into a "corporate" position with Uber. While filling out the information requested, the questions started to seem a little odd. I literally said out loud to my computer, "What am I applying for?!" It turned out to be for an Uber *Driver!* Well, I knew someone who was doing that on the side so I thought, *why not me?!* – My customers got the biggest kick out of my Accidental Uber Driver story. It was easy, great extra $$, and I was able to network while I was looking for a job! Multi-win mishap that turned out to be – *uber fun*.

#86 Rent a Jon Boat or Pontoon

You do not have to be a pro to enjoy a day on the lake. Renting a small boat is a wonderful way to get fresh air, enjoy time in nature, and spend a day on the water. My fav? Renting a pontoon to celebrate our family birthdays. Picnic lunch, balloons, gifts, and birthday cake with all of our names on it! – #BirthdayBoatBash

#87 Check Out a Dating App

Even if this is not your ideal way of meeting someone, I can confirm there are genuinely nice men using dating apps. Granted they are slipped between the crazy ones, but nice nonetheless. (Just be sure you've read Chapters 10 and 11 first!) If you've been hesitant about getting back into the dating world, this may be a great way to re-enter with minimal commitment or exposure and you can usually create a free profile to check out a dating site.

Note: If you have to input bank info to get started, be sure to check the *Do Not Renew* box. That little mistake cost me $120 once – and gave me enough story for another book! Worst case? If you don't meet anyone worth dating, you will at least have several weeks of laughter viewing those who are off the charts. Go sneak a peak!

#88 Take a Job with Travel

For a spell of my life, I couldn't justify spending money on travel. I did, however, learn to create mini-vacations out of business travel! When I had conferences, I always built in something to either sightsee or experience a different culture. On one work trip, I booked my return flight out of a different airport, took some extra days, and drove up the eastern coast which I had never seen. Shoot for the stars. – You might get to tour the moon!

#89 Try a Different Hairstyle

Does your hairstyle look the same as it did 20 years ago? It might be time for a new do! Pick a good salon with the know-how. It will be worth the investment finding a quality stylist. If you can swing it, indulge in a new styling product, too! This is a sure fire way to start my day with a smile. There is such a thing as a *Good Hair Day!*

#90 Experience a Theater

Find a performing arts theater close to your area. It makes for a fun night to dress up and take in a theater production. If you have a friend who can go with you, great! If not, enjoy it alone. Chances are, there will be someone beside you who will be happy to chat between the acts.

#91 Volunteer in Your Business Organization

For years I held positions or worked on project groups through my HR organization (SHRM). It was an easy way to network, make friends, and build my resume. Great memories. Wins all the way around!

#92 Visit an Aquarium

Even if you have to drive some hours for the visit, an aquarium makes for a great day trip. Alone or with a friend, it is both a unique and peaceful experience. For an extra special treat, dining at an Aquarium restaurant is a unique experience for the memory book!

#93 Work Night Out

When I was younger, a group of us would meet once a week after work. Our boss never joined us, but her husband always got there first to reserve the tables. Then there was always someone with a corny joke to share. Those are days of irreplaceable memories and friendships that have lasted through the years. Maybe you start your own work night tradition. If not weekly, you could start with a holiday or sport season to kick it off.

#94 Get Your Degree

One of my life goals was to get my master's degree. It is one of the hardest things I've done yet a reward like no other! Beyond the accomplishment, it led to promotion and an amazing career. Is it maybe your time for education? You're never too old! At one point, I was in college the same time as my kids. – Don't worry, different universities!

#95 Plant a Tree

Yes, you can! I once planted a small dogwood not knowing at all what to expect. And guess what?! It grew! You basically dig a hole, add garden soil, and water it! It will dress up your yard and it gives you something to feel proud of. As I'm writing this, I'm crossing my fingers for two small citrus trees I recently planted. Tangelos for snacks. Limes for summer drinks and ice water!

#96 Take a Cruise

Am I suggesting you take a cruise alone? Well, yes, if there's no one to go with you. I did this once and it was incredibly refreshing! There are always deals available and you can start with a 2-3 night excursion. By the way, if you do happen to try it alone, you will not be the only solo cruiser. There are singles cruises, as well as dinner dining and events for others sailing sans partner. – Bon Voyage!

#97 Host a Theme Party

Have a friend with an upcoming birthday? A theme party with costumes is easy, loads of fun to plan, and your guests will enjoy getting in the spirit with you. This makes for a great surprise party, as well. I've done period parties, vintage circus, and lots of kids parties. Dress up and make some memories!

#98 Ride a Bike

Biking is a great way to get some fresh air and see parts of your community you might not otherwise notice. If you want to go all out with it, cities often have greenways where you can really venture the outdoors! p.s. I highly recommend investing in a pair of bike shorts!

#99 Get Certified in Something

Whether this means First Aid or a professional designation in your career, working toward a certification is rewarding and gives you something worthwhile to focus on. I've had two HR Certifications in the past and later worked to become a Certified Life Coach. The accomplishment is a definite energy boost!

#100 Join a Local Charity

A sure way to lift your spirits is to give of yourself to a worthy cause. It's easy to search the internet for opportunities in your city. I used to volunteer for Operation Stand Down in Nashville helping retired veterans transition over to civilian jobs. It allowed me to do good while using skills I already had. 'So rewarding and a way to give back to my country.

#101 The *Single Ticket* Advantage

Generally, I agree bigger excursions are more fun with a partner. That said, they are also more expensive! This might be a good time in your life to consider a venture when it's just a *single* ticket you're purchasing. I once indulged like this during a business convention. One afternoon, I slipped away and took a helicopter tour into the Grand Canyon, complete with a landing and picnic dinner *in the canyon!* My trip was scheduled with the nicest older couple – who had no issues dropping hints trying to fix me up with the pilot during our little excursion. While that was somewhat embarrassing, I have to admit I enjoyed a couple dates with him during my stay. All kidding aside, that helicopter tour was one for the record books. Absolutely gorgeous and amazing!

Dream Your Greenhouse

If these ideas sound far beyond what you can imagine for your life right now, I want to encourage you still to set goals for those special plans you have! This will give you a positive focus and fun energy to boost your spirits. I can't express enough how many opportunities are out there waiting for you and could be closer than you think! I want to share one last story of how little plans can turn into big dreams...

Do you remember I mentioned one year I hosted our office Christmas party? I had just moved into a new house and I thought it would be a fun way to let everyone see my new home. And of course, I wanted to give everyone a tour!

Well, in that home, I had a bonus room upstairs. (In Tennessee we often have these over our garages instead of basements.) This particular bonus room was the biggest one I certainly ever had. In fact, I didn't even have it fully furnished because I couldn't afford to spend any more dollars at the time. But one piece I *knew* I wanted up there was a pool table! Even though I couldn't afford one, it was still my dream for that room. One night, a few weeks before the office party, my kids came over and they helped me decide where this future pool table should go. We had so much fun finding measurements, talking angles, and creating spacing for the best pool shots. Once we had the location figured out, we put blue painters tape down on the carpet marking the perfect future spot of our new pool table!

Not many weeks later, then, I had my office Christmas party. When I gave the grand tour and reached the bonus room, everyone was of course curious about the blue tape on the carpet. They all got the biggest laugh when I told them it was *my pool table!*

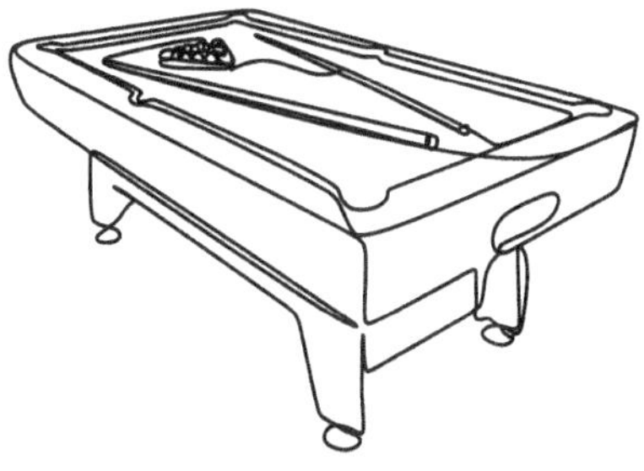

A few days later, however, one of my co-workers from the party asked if I would be interested in a used pool table for my bonus room! (Well, yes, and it would depend on the price, condition, the style, etc.) Then she clarified. It was nice and it would be *free.* Her in-laws were clearing their basement and they would GIVE me their pool table! – Along with all the accessories: sticks, balls, chalks, and games. All I had to do was pay to have it removed.

I found a company who removed the table from their house, delivered and installed it in mine, *and* placed a brand new felt covering on it – all for $200!!! Not only did I get my new pool table, I was also able to choose the color to match my decor!

When I set out that blue painters tape for my future pool table, I had no idea when I would ever be able to actually afford a purchase that large. But I knew I wanted it and it was fun to plan with my kids. That simple act and silly tape allowed my dream to come to reality in a way I could not have ever imagined!

This is why I want you to dream. This is why I want you to plan. Never underestimate your dreams – or who might cross your path to bring them to reality!

NEXT STEPS

Something to think about...

When is the last time you dreamed of doing something big for yourself? You do know you deserve it. You do know almost anything is possible, right?

Something to move forward...

Schedule a quiet moment, or take a pause right now. Breathe in deeply. Hold. Exhale. Stop. Dream. What is your dream? Write it in your journal.

Something to do...

Open your eyes and ears. Tomorrow look around your world (or search the bigger world) for that dream you have. Then start to prepare. Even if it's simply tucking back a $1 bill toward the expense, asking someone for advice, or searching the internet.

Get ready. Go build your greenhouse!

16

It Started Over Coffee

I don't remember much about the story, but years ago I saw a movie with the song, "I Finally Found Someone." If you haven't heard it, I encourage you to go have a listen [Adams & Streisand]. The words of that song have always stayed with me, I think in a very *wishful* kind of way. It made me want for a moment like that. An unexpected kind of experience. One that was undeniable. That moment where I would find my *someone* over a simple cup of coffee.

I am all too familiar, though, with those periods living alone where you give up thinking there will ever be that special someone come into your life. I was recently talking with a friend about how long my single years had been. She laughed, "If that happened to me, I would be 83!!" While it was rather funny, I am confident that will not happen to her! I dearly hope for my friend. And I dearly hope for you, too. I hope you will one day have your started-over-coffee moment that leads to your *finally* relationship in life.

As much as we might wish for it, though, that moment does not always show up on our time clock. I know the days of loneliness can turn into weeks, and the weeks can turn into months. I also know that months can turn into years. At a certain point, you begin to wonder if this is life. If there will never be an invite for a cup of coffee. If there will ever be *someone*. – That's the reason I wrote this book. I want to encourage you in these periods, however long they might be. I want you to know you are definitely not alone.

> Wishing for the cup of coffee that turns into something, is *real*. It's very real.

Let me encourage you, though. If you have given up on the idea of ever finding someone, the reality is, one day you might! You may discover your someone has been right under your nose all along. – Or your lives could suddenly cross very unexpectedly. I had a college friend who met her husband one day in a horrendously long traffic jam on the highway! (And he was a cutie, I might add.) While there may be no guarantee for us to find a partner, there is certainly *always* the possibility!

I know it can feel like your chances are slim. However, I also know that one single random conversation can turn your life completely around. And when that random conversation happens, I want for you to be ready!

These last pages are here to help you prepare for that moment. To process. To *really* process. With eyes open. Practical. So you can be prepared realistically. They say love is blind. That may be true, but quite frankly, I enjoy life a whole lot more when I have my contacts in! So while I do want for you to find a wonderful loving experience, I also want for you to be ready for it! Because it may happen in a blink, in a random interaction, when you're least expecting it. I had this happen to me once... and I wasn't ready.

It was simply one ordinary night walking out after work. I needed to drop a note into someone's box so I took the front stairs rather than my usual back exit. Walking through our lobby, I overheard my boss discussing a client with our receptionist and I chimed in to the conversation. That one conversation led to my boss having the idea to give my number to this single client of ours. The man was quite wealthy and I thought, "This date will make for a great story to tell one day!" (I mean, we're talking real life *Pretty Woman* date – minus the prostitute part, of course, but you get my gist.) I then jokingly offered my number.

Well, much to my surprise, our "cup of coffee" (aka dinner) eventually led to him falling for me. I was truly loved and cherished. I was also inexperienced and unsure. Bottom line, I was not at all prepared. And I made the decision to not marry him. Our deep care for each other continued and that man never stopped loving me. It continued to his last days and I was the person he wanted to be with in his final months. Even though I never did marry him, the entire experience of our years together taught me something invaluable that I will never forget. From that very day I said, "Okay," and gave my number, I have carried the lesson I learned. I even created my own *quote* from it! And I want to pass the encouragement on to you:

"You never know what a day might bring forth!"

That unique experience showed me our cup-of-coffee moment can happen at any time. It can start from any random conversation. Your *someone* experience may be initiated from a different walk you take as you're leaving work. It might start with a smile. A simple dinner. A laugh. A chemistry you're not expecting.

I had a very simple task, *to place a note in a mailbox.* I agreed to one fun night out. And that one ordinary incident changed my life on multiple levels (for which there are not enough pages in this book). I accept now that I was not prepared. It's okay that he did not end up being my ultimate someone. It was that random way we met and the experience I had which gave me the hope and confidence I have now to know *anything* can happen in our lives! Mine – and yours!! The experience taught me that love truly *can* start over a simple, random cup of coffee for us. And when it does, we want to be ready.

Cream or Sugar?

After that relationship, life settled in. My career became involved, and I eventually adjusted to the ups and downs of being single again. My preference, though? It was always *definitely* married life. I wanted a partner. I was personally cut out for that lifestyle. I knew marriage was what I ultimately wanted.

There was just one issue, though, of which I was not aware when my single years began. In my mind (I realize now), I had only snippets of what being married again actually might look like. And when I say snippets, I mean snippets.

Snippets: Clips. *Pieces*. Bits. *Morsels*.

Even when I stepped into serious relationships and *thought* I wanted to get married again, I'm not sure I fully pictured how differently a new married life might look from how it was in my past – or how it currently looked in my mind! When I married the first time, we were young and life was just starting out. When you meet later in life, though?? Well, there is a bit more to blend than just cream 'n sugar when you meet later in life! Thus, the desire to offer you these final pages.

Do I want to encourage you through my writing? Yes! I want you to know there are possibilities and your cup of coffee may be waiting in the next coffee shop! I also want you have a realistic expectation of what that coffee experience might look like. Obviously, when you think you've met someone, the two of you will enjoy spending time together. Your Top 10 Guide will have ensured the similar values are present. You'll have checked the big boxes like finances, career, intellect, and your spiritual life. I'm fairly certain there will be a mutual physical attraction.

With all of those pieces coming together, it might sound like you would be ready for Prince Macchiato to sweep you back to his castle! – I was there, too. What I had *not* however realized was that, while I was living my single life, my life had changed in little ways. And where I had thought through all the big life items, I had not considered the importance of some of the smaller ones. Thus enters the thoughts on *Cream or Sugar*.

If you have not yet noticed, when living single we have the flexibility to do things *our way*. It doesn't take long for our personal preferences to take root, because there is no one interfering. No one asking us to do it differently. If I prefer my towels to be folded a certain way, I get to enjoy my neatly organized closets. If I like my spices to be alphabetized, I will always know where to find the paprika!

It's also rather nice to keep my own schedule. If I want to sleep extra minutes on Saturday or stay up late watching a rom-com, it's my prerogative! I can wait to throw my clothes in the washer on Saturday because I know I have enough panties to last two weeks! My life might be chaotic sometimes, but it's mine and I'm making it work for me. On my terms. *Are you with me?*

Now, not to burst your cappuccino bubbles, but I want to point out how our visions for marriage and the actual arrival of Prince Macchiato might struggle lining up when that moment happens and real life hits. Whether you like it or not, you have probably begun to relax a little into the single life you've created for yourself. It's not a bad thing; however, it is definitely a thing. You've heard people talk about being set in their ways, right? Even if you think that's not you. (You see yourself as being easy and flexible.) You are probably a bit more set than you might realize. That's all okay. I just want to make sure you are aware of it and to help you prepare for Prince M's arrival into your life.

Allow me to illustrate how this might play out. I know I certainly had the marriage vision and I could absolutely picture my future life! Do you see it? It's Friday night and you're snuggled up on your sofa under the squishy blanket watching movies together. Hallmark rom-com, sharing popcorn from your red 'n white striped popcorn bowl. (I don't even own a red 'n white striped bowl but that's what my envisioned husband and I were always eating popcorn out of.) On Saturday afternoon, the sun is shining through the beautiful trees as he's walking beside you on your hiking trail. You're meandering the Farmers Market with locked arms enjoying the displays. And of course the bedroom life is always seamless. There's a solid income stream. Mutual respect and affection... *This* is what married life is and this is what you're ready for.

In my favorite thought, I was always standing at the stove making spaghetti, wooden spoon in hand, stirring my sauce in the pot. He comes up behind me, wraps his arms around my waist, and kisses the top of my head. *Mmm.* – I have no idea where that visual of a fantasy came from, but I always thought that would be the ultimate life partner.

It never dawned on me, though, that *maybe* my life partner would not like spaghetti. Or *maybe* my husband would be practical and prefer helping in the kitchen rather than showing affection at the stove top. Or... maybe he would have his *own* sauce recipe and I would not be making the spaghetti at all!!

In my snippet, *An Evening in the Married Life of Michelle*, I had pictured life with my future husband based on the mold I had created in my mind. Then I had to ask myself, "Where did that mold come from??" My mold of a man, I have to think, was very likely influenced from that Top Ten List I had created. My little kitchen dream didn't have to include conversation about football because that was a given... as was his height... and his clothing... and our social life. He fit into my mold and I was content. And they lived happily ever after. *The End.*

Okay, perhaps I didn't completely expect my actual Prince Macchiato to come riding up to the coffee shop on his white stallion. However, I have to admit I was guilty of picturing how *alike* we were, rather than how different certain things in our everyday lives might be. I drink my coffee with a little creamer. It never dawned on me that I might one day see my partner adding two entire packets of yellow sweetener to his cup of Joe! Eww. (That makes my tongue curl thinking about it.) I didn't picture there may come a time when my night owl tendencies would have to adjust to someone needing more sleep than me. Or that I would ever have a partner who doesn't consider black a color, when black, gray and white make up the entire core palette of my wardrobe! The little differences? I had not considered them. I had my list, my mold. And for some reason, my partner always seemed to fit neat and tidy into the married life of my envisioned future.

Preferring cream versus sugar. Sleeping in or barely sleeping. A little messy or a lot tidy. Even though these characteristics may not rise to the Top 10 level, they *can* have a Top 10 impact if we've not realistically considered how they might fit into our lifestyle. They are neither good nor bad; however, they will be present. And though these subtle differences don't fit pretty into our fairy tale visions, it will behoove us to be ready for them.

What if He Likes Tea?

A few chapters ago, I encouraged you to create that list of qualities you would like in a partner. Whether or not you physically created your Top Ten List of traits, I think it's safe to say most of us have a certain *type* of person in mind for our future. (Being transparent here, I never veered from Item #6 *Must love football!*) Maybe you have priorities around character qualities, hobbies, physical appearance, or a certain motivational level. A list like this is a solid tool to keep you levelheaded in seeking someone compatible to your core tastes and values. I still believe this list is important to guide us. Where I do want to encourage you now, is in taking the next step to process what life might look like when there are differences!

When you do meet someone, your list has likely prepared you to pick up on all the similarities between the two of you. These similarities provide a comfort level and the ability to naturally enjoy time together. It's easy to date him because you have so much in common and a comfortable pattern will develop.

As you further get to know him, however, the differences between the two of you will begin to show a little more than you initially noticed. Realistically, one day those differences might begin to annoy you. Some of them may not be as cute or funny as they were in the first few dates. Other differences might be polar opposite to how you've done things all your life and it could be a bit of an adjustment.

Becoming aware of these subtle differences is not at all to say this is a bad thing! It is, though, a time to pause and take yourself through an exercise in honesty. Those differences you see? Tea, and not coffee? Early bird versus night owl? This is where your dreams and lists meet everyday life. This is when you have your own heart-to-heart reflection. It's neither good nor bad. It's you having a get-real with yourself. It's when you say, "This is not what I pictured." Then, you evaluate: Am I being too particular? Or is this going to be a constant challenge? Can I adjust? Can I ask *them* to adjust?! Are my expectations too high? – There is no right or wrong to these questions. The right or wrong here lies within you being able to be honest with yourself and then talking with your partner about it.

Your partner is going to have quirks. They will do things differently. There may be a few boxes unchecked. If you begin to notice this, that's a good sign. This means love has not blinded you and you are proceeding with a level head! It's not so much about the differences themselves, but rather what are you doing with them?

When challenging differences surface, you should be able to have a conversation about them. (This is where the younger me failed. I didn't know how to talk through it, so I got frustrated and left.) If you can't reach some compromise together, that's when the differences should lead to evaluating if this person is your *someone*. On the other hand, if you can work through them, embrace the variety! And who knows, you may learn to like tea just as much as coffee!

Coffee Shops

When I think of coffee shops, I see people meeting together. Enjoying time with each other. Enjoying something in common – their love of coffee. Coffee shops are a great source for community. They provide a warm, comfortable place for people to come together.

Just like the environment in a coffee shop, there will come a time in your new budding relationship when you will want to provide that warm environment for *your* community, your friends and family, to come together to meet your special someone. To this point, you will have had dates and personal time together. Most likely there will be hours of conversation clocked between the two of you. You will have discovered your compatibility and all you share in common. Your friends and family will have undoubtedly heard all about this new person… and they will be ever so curious to meet him!

When the day arrives, bear in mind they will have *heard* all about your new beau, but this will be their first actual in-person experience with him. They may be excited and hopeful for you. And they will also most likely be present with a protective eye! Hopefully, all goes well. If, on the other hand, your friends or family have questions or concerns, it will be wise to consider their opinion. It could be as simple as explaining something they may not know; or it could be a question you need to discuss on your next date.

> Remember, your friends and family have known you longer. They may be seeing something you're *not*.

Beyond the actual questions or concerns from your group, it is also important to observe the dynamic of how they interact together. You may be completely smitten with this person, but the reality is they are an addition to your community. (Your community who knows you best and has been your support system for a long time.) If the two worlds struggle to blend, you may need to step back and evaluate how the relationship will work in the future. Remember, your friends and family are your circle. They are your coffee shop in life. Warmth. Familiarity. The ones who offer a comfortable place for you. If they see your new date blending into their group, that's a good sign you're headed in the right direction.

If you discover, though, too many differences for your comfort, unanswered questions, or not a good blending of communities, you may have to evaluate if it's the best relationship to continue. I know when you date someone who seems to be *the one,* it is heartbreaking to experience hope and then loss if it doesn't work. The loss, however, is much better than getting yourself locked into an unhealthy situation. If that does happen? Remember this: When you become available again – *The door is wide open to accept a fresh cup of coffee!*

Finally Meeting Someone

It's very likely your day *will* come when you do meet your someone. It will not feel forced and there will be nothing you can do to mess it up. Will there be some compromise? Yes, of course. Will there be differences? Occasional tiffs? Yes, that's human nature. Will there be misunderstandings? Yes, and you will forgive and grow through them. Will there also be fun and compatibility? Yes, there will!

I have wanted this book to be realistic and focused solely on you, so I have refrained from telling my personal story. However, after decades single again, I very randomly met my incredible husband. *You never know what a day might bring forth!* When you least expect or believe it can, your cup-of-coffee moment truly can happen! I hope this for you and I pray this for you. It may not be anywhere near the time table you have in your mind. Trust me on this, that is OKAY! It is much better to wait and be with the right person. When you find your someone, he will make these lonely years disappear. And you will make his lonely years disappear, too.

For now, have fun, stay level-headed, be smart, and be prepared. Your future self will thank you. There is, in this moment, so much of meaningful life and growth ahead for you.

While researching this chapter, I surprisingly discovered many incredible correlations between *coffee* and the single woman. I seriously could not have found any better words for my final thoughts. These last pages are my gift of encouragement I leave with you...

In the coffee shop of life there is the coffee pot...
and then there is the *Cafetière à Piston!*
A French Press; a *single* cup!

Cafetière à Piston

A French Press. "Single Cup" of coffee.

As much as you might wish to have your moment where you can say it *started over coffee*, and as much as I think it is very wise to be prepared for that possibility in life, right now you are here. You are living and navigating solo life. You are a single cup of coffee, a true *cafetière à piston*.

By the way, if you're a coffee drinker, this might be a great time to go make yourself a cup and curl in! Go ahead. I'll wait. Better yet, I'm going to fix a cup of coffee, myself! I made banana muffins this morning and they've been waiting on the counter all day for me. I'll see you in a few minutes.

...I'm back. And the muffin? It pairs perfectly with my Pike's Roast which, coincidentally, I'm drinking in my Pike's Peak coffee mug. There is definitely something special about sitting alone savoring a cup of coffee. It pulls me in, gives me pause, and I feel like it's that moment where I can take a break from the rest of the world.

If you're not a coffee fan, please know the following words of encouragement *still* apply! This chapter is not really about coffee. It started with the song, and the song about coffee just happened to allow me to discover some very real correlations to navigating the single life. As soon as I got the idea of creating a chapter to guide you when you meet that special person, the song, "I Finally Found Someone," immediately came to mind and I knew I wanted to use it for my background. It's not so much that I love coffee, rather I love the message in the song. And I love the relationship that started over a simple cup of coffee. Thus, the analogies across these pages.

Researching then how I might leverage the coffee topic, I stumbled across the phrase *Cafetière à Piston*. Since I am not brushed up on my French language, I wanted to check out what exactly that phrase meant.

Ahhh, I love it! It's how the French say "French Press." And that's how I learned that the unique benefits of a single cup of French Press coffee are exactly the qualities and benefits you have in being a *single person*. Here are the characteristics I discovered...

Superior Flavor & Body. *The process of the French Press allows oils and fine particles to remain in the brew, resulting in a stronger, richer texture.*

As a single person, there are going to be times when every fiber of your being might feel the pressure coming down around you. It will not feel great when it's happening, but the result is that your character is being built by these challenging times. This can be an incredible period of self-reflection and growth. A time where you can see exactly how strong you are. The pressures in life are never very comfortable when they're happening; however, you will come through this experience with a *richer texture* to your being. This is a period in life to appreciate. It's an opportunity for growing into a stronger person. Pressing forward and finding your inner strength will result in a life of superior flavor!

Simplicity: *It is easy to use; no need for electricity or complicated equipment.*

Simple may be anything except how you would describe your life right now. While it may not feel simple at the moment, allow me to contrast the alternative. In life, we are going to face problems, married or not. As a single person, though, you more often have the freedom to pick and choose how you want to handle those problems. I'll use the budget as an example, because I imagine that's a topic near and dear to your heart.

When money is tight and I live alone, I can be completely content with a bowl of Cheerios for breakfast, a bag of Steamfresh vegetables for lunch, and a small chicken breast with salad for dinner. Snacks? Add almonds, cheese sticks, and a handful of M&Ms. Well under $10 for the day. Repeat with different veggies tomorrow. In a pinch, I can make this work. Actually, in a pinch I *have* made this work! Simplicity. No need for complicated equipment.

Is it the most fun way to eat? No, absolutely not. However, I can make those food choices for myself and keep my budget simple because it's just me. I understand if you have kids you may need to throw in PB&J and a bag of popcorn from time to time. However, do you see? There's no one pressuring you to overspend. It's your budget, no arguments about buying more at the grocery store. No juggling bills because you overspent based on someone else's pressure. You can keep things as simple as you need or want. I am the queen of simple and I love it. Quite honestly, there have been nights when my fluffy robe, dollar popcorn, and Netflix sure beat dressing up, fixing makeup, and trotting about town. Nights on the town are fun; however, when I need to watch my dollars, it's nice being able to choose a simple, inexpensive night at home whenever I want!

Control: *The brewer has full control over the immersion time and strength.*

When you live alone, your life is your life and you have complete control over it. Even if you feel like there are times when you are spinning out of control, the reality is, YOU can decide if you want to spin down that path. Have I had overwhelming moments where my life didn't feel so in control?

Umm, YES. Just months after my divorce, I had a horrific accident where a buck came through my windshield, totaled my car, and ripped off the left side of my face. That led to a 2-year ordeal of specialty visits, plastic surgeries, and a restructure of my nose and eyelids.

Later, I was in college at one point during the same time my kids were in college. Later still, I had a pipe break in my upstairs. The flooding caused my house to be gutted to the frame, and I was out of my home for 6 months that year. Not long after, my son-in-law passed away. That was the same day my new baby granddaughter turned 7 weeks old.

These events don't include the jobs lost due to restructures. My teen's car accidents. Putting down our poodle. Or my house that got destroyed by a renter. My other 2 major surgeries. Or being diagnosed with Meniere's disease.

I *know* what it's like to feel my *world* spinning out of control. However, in every situation, I had the ability to take control, to seek help where I needed it, and to decide that I was going to hang in there and not allow my situation to control me! As a single person, you get to do that.

> It's your life.
> You get to choose what you want to do with it.

Versatility: *It can be used for making cold brew or for steeping tea.*

'Speaking of choosing what you want to do, this is your opportunity to be versatile! Your single life is your single life. What do you want to do with it? Where do you want to navigate?! Do you want to try something new? Do you want to get your education? Do you want to reinvent yourself? Do you want to move?? – I have a good single friend who wanted to move to Portugal... *and so she did!!*

This is your time, and your time alone. Take advantage of it! You don't like coffee? Switch over to tea. Is tea too boring? Try a boba tea! If you feel like you are stuck and can't figure out how to break your cycle, talk to a friend about it. Talk to your pastor. Seek a Life Coach who can help you see what potential might be out there for you. This is your time. The world is yours! Go make it whatever you want it to be.

Durability: *French presses can last for many years.*

I believe this is my overall favorite characteristic of the French press. Durable. This is you. When you think you can't, *yes you can!* As a single person, you are building a strength within yourself that is not easily matched. The single life is not for the faint of heart. It's a life which coupled people cannot fully understand. It's a world which requires inner strength every single day. Every single day you will face a challenge. Every single day you will grow stronger. Every day you figure it out. Every day you exude durability.

You are *Durable*. Tough. Resilient. Secure. Strong. Stable. Indestructible. This is you. You got this. You can do this. You *can* navigate the single life.

–You are the ultimate Cafetière à Piston

NEXT STEPS

Something to think about...

How would you feel if you discovered a new relationship has *started over coffee?*

Something to move forward...

What fairy tale picture of marriage have you envisioned that you may need to alter when you think you have finally found your someone?

Something to do...

Which character trait of the French Press do you most closely relate? In your journal, write down positive phrases that describe you or character qualities you would like to grow in your life.

You are enough. No pixie dust required.

Credits

Graphic art designed by Freepik/Magnific.

Michelle Bridges Harper is happily retired after spending a full career in Corporate America. After decades of coaching leaders, she now pursues her passion for writing and encouraging others. Michelle holds her Masters Degree in Management and has become a Certified Life Coach.

Michelle spent 28 years of single-again life in middle Tennessee and is now living out her retirement plan on the Gulf Coast with her husband, Chris. Michelle enjoys time with family, hosting parties, landscaping her yard, and is an avid DIYer. Her dream would be to have her own HGTV show, renovating homes on a budget! She also has a big sense of humor and is satisfied letting that dream be a dream. When she and Chris are not traveling, you can find them kicking back with a bowl of popcorn, experimenting in the kitchen, or meandering the white breezy Florida beaches.

Available for Life Coaching and speaking engagements.
Visit: www.MountainMoveConsulting.com

www.ingramcontent.com/pod-product-compliance
Lightning Source LLC
Chambersburg PA
CBHW070249130726
48054CB00022B/160

* 9 7 9 8 9 9 0 3 8 2 3 9 8 *